TUTTO *a mano*

Acknowledgements

Editorial Director Davd Codling

Editor and Graphic Design Gregory Courtney

Photography Kathryn Martin

Photo Editing Steve Ernnez

Clothing Cicada Collection, Santa Fe

Buttons Renaissance/Blue Moon Buttons

Jewelry Bash, _www.bashsf.com_

Styling, Hair & Makeup Mary Jonatis

Models Katy Ashmann, Grace Anna Farrow & Julia Hoffman

Location Thanks Cicada Collection, _www.cicadacollection.com_ and Arrediamo, _www.arrediamo.com_

Color Reproduction & Printing Regent Publishing Services

Published and Distributed by TUTTO Santa Fe

Printed in China

ISBN 0-9752931-3-3

17 knitting patterns featuring
an eclectic mix of designers and yarns.

Table of Contents

Textured Vest

rustic texture in a vintage style   gregory courtney

MEASUREMENTS
Chest 37½ (42, 44¼ 48¾)".
Length 23 (24, 25, 26)".
Length to Underarm 14½ (15, 15½, 16)".
Armhole Depth 8½ (9, 9½, 10)".

YARN
Isager Highland: 100 (100, 150, 150) grams each of Color A and Color B. Shown in Color A, Scots Pine and Color B, Sage Blue.

NEEDLES
24" circular US 2 (2.75 mm) and US 3 (3.25 mm); 16" circular US 2. *Adjust needle sizes to obtain gauge.*

NOTIONS
5 stitch holders. Stitch markers. Locking stitch marker or safety pin.

GAUGE
28 sts and 40 rows = 4" in **Main Body Pattern**.

BAND PATTERN (MULTIPLE OF 4 STS + 3 STS)
CO with Color A.

Foundation Row (WS): With Color A, *k1, p1; rep from * to last st; end k1.
Row 1 (RS) With Color B, *p1, k1, p1, slip 1 wyib; rep from * to last 3 sts; end p1, k1, p1.
Row 2 With Color B, *k1, p1, k1, slip 1 wyif; rep from * to last 3 sts; end k1, p1, k1.
Row 3 With Color A, *p1, k1; rep from * to last st; end p1.

Row 4 With Color A, *k1, p1; rep from * to last st; end k1.

Rep Rows 1-4.

MAIN BODY PATTERN (MULTIPLE OF 4 STS + 3 STS)
Row 1 (RS) With Color B, *p1, k1; rep from * to last st; end p1.
Row 2 With Color B, *p1, k1; rep from * to last st; end p1.
Row 3 With Color A, *p1, k1, p1, slip 1 wyib; rep from * to last 3 sts; end p1, k1, p1.
Row 4 With Color A, *p1, k1, p1, slip 1 wyif; rep from * to last 3 sts; end p1, k1, p1.

Rep Rows 1-4.

VEST
BACK
With 24" US 2, CO 131 (147, 155, 171) sts. Work in **Band Pattern** until piece measures 2 (2½, 2½, 2½)" from CO edge. Change to 24" circular US 3 and work **Main Body Pattern** until piece measures 14½ (15, 15½, 16)" from CO edge, ending after working row 4 of pattern.

SHAPE UNDERARMS
Next Row (RS) BO first 12 sts in pattern; work next 107 (123, 131, 147) sts in pattern as set; BO last 12 sts in pattern. Break Color B.

Rejoin Color B and work WS row.

TUTTO *a mano* 9

TEXTURED VEST

Break off Color A, rejoin and continue in pattern as set, **AND AT SAME TIME**, dec 1 st at beg and end of every RS row 8 (8, 8, 8) times. Continue without further shaping on rem 91 (107, 115, 131) sts until piece measures 22¾ (23¾, 24¾, 25¾)" from CO edge, ending after working Row 2 of pattern.

SHAPE BACK NECK
Next Row (RS) (row 3 of pattern) Work 19 (27, 31, 39) sts in pattern.

Turn and work row 4 of pattern as set. Break yarn and place these 19 (27, 31, 39) sts on holder for right shoulder. Place next 53 (53, 53, 53) sts onto another holder for back neck. Rejoin Color A and work row 3 (RS) of pattern on rem 19 (27, 31, 39) sts, then work row 4 (WS). Break yarn and place sts on holder for left shoulder.

FRONT
Work same as for front through underarm shaping, ending after working a WS row.

SHAPE FRONT NECK
Next Row (RS) Work 43 (51, 55, 63) sts, k2tog or p2tog as appropriate for pattern, work next st and place on locking stitch marker or safety pin, k2tog or p2tog as appropriate for pattern, work rem 43 (51, 55, 63) sts.

Turn, and working each side separately, breaking and reattaching yarn when needed, dec 1 st at neck edge every 2nd row (11, 9, 7, 5) times, then every 4th row 14 (16, 18, 20) times. Continue in pattern as set without further shaping on rem 19 (27, 31, 39) sts until same length as back, ending after working row 4 of pattern. Place sts on holders for shoulders.

JOIN SHOULDERS & SEW SIDE SEAMS

With Color B, RS's facing each other and WS facing you, join shoulders using 3-needle bind-off method. Sew side seams up to underarm.

NECKBAND

With 16" circular US 2 and Color A, beg at right shoulder seam, pick up 4 (4, 4, 4) sts up to back neck holder, k53 (53, 53, 53) sts from back neck holder, pick up 4 (4, 4, 4) sts to left shoulder seam, pick up 73 (77, 81, 85) sts along left neck edge, knit the st from safety pin, pick up 73 (77, 81, 85) sts along right neck edge to shoulder seam—208 (216, 224, 232) sts on needle.

NOTE When working pattern rnds for neckband, you won't necessarily end up with a full rep before working decs at neck center. After working decs, work a mirror image of pattern on opposite side of neckband.

Mark st previously on safety pin with locking stitch marker or safety pin so you know this is your front center st. Place marker for beg of rnd and work in the rnd as follows:

Set-up Rnd With Color A, *k1, p1; rep from * to end of rnd.
Rnds 1 & 2 With Color B, *slip 1 pwise wyib, k1, p1, k1; rep from * to 2 sts before marked st at front center, ssk, knit marked st, k2tog, continue pattern as established to end of rnd.
Rnds 3 & 4 With Color A, *k1, p1; rep from * to 2 sts before marked st at front center, ssk, knit marked st, k2tog, continue pattern as established to end of rnd. Rep Rnds 1-4 until neckband measures 1¼ (1¼, 1¼, 1¼)", ending after working rnd 4 of pattern. With Color A, BO in knit.

ARMBANDS

With 16" circular US 2 and Color A, beg at center seam of underarm, pick up 72 (76, 80, 84) sts evenly along armhole edge to shoulder seam, 1 st at shoulder seam and 71 (75, 79, 83) sts along armhole edge to underarm—144 (152, 160, 168) sts on needle. Place marker for beg of rnd and work in the rnd as follows:

Set-Up Rnd With Color A, *k1, p1; rep from * to end of rnd.
Rnds 1 & 2 With Color B, *k1, p1, slip 1 pwise wyib, p1; rep from * to end of rnd.
Rnds 3 & 4 With Color A, *k1, p1; rep from * to end of rnd.

Rep rnds 1-4 until armband measures 1¼ (1¼, 1¼, 1¼)", ending after working rnd 4 of pattern. With Color A, BO in knit.

FINISHING

Weave in ends. Block gently.

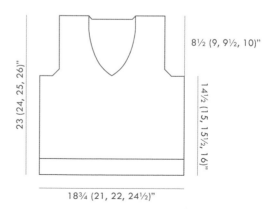

8½ (9, 9½, 10)"

23 (24, 25, 26)"

14½ (15, 15½, 16)"

18¾ (21, 22, 24½)"

Short Jacket

smart style in brioche and garter stitch   marianne isager

MEASUREMENTS
Chest 39½ (42½, 45¾)".
Length 19¾ (21¾, 23¾)".
Length to Underarm 11½ (13, 14½)".
Armhole Depth 8¼ (8¾, 9¼)".
Sleeve Length 17¾ (19, 20)".

YARN
250 (300, 300) grams of Isager Highland.
250 (300, 300) grams of Isager Alpaca 2.

Shown in Highland Thistle and Alpaca 2 #2105 (lt. natural gray).

Hold 1 strand of Highland and 1 strand of Alpaca 2 together throughout.

NEEDLES
US 4 (3.5 mm). *Adjust needle size to obtain gauge.*

NOTIONS
Two ¾ –1" diameter buttons. Locking stitch markers and stitch holders.

GAUGE
Average of 20 sts and 44 rows = 4" x 4" on US 4 in combination of brioche st and garter st.

GAUGE SWATCH
Besides being a gauge swatch, this swatch provides practice for the brioche/garter st combination and also the slipped edge used on the lapel.

With 1 strand of Highland and 1 strand of Alpaca 2 held together throughout, CO 20 sts.

In the brioche sections, don't count the yo's in the st counts.

Set-up Row (RS) ([Yo, slip 1 pwise, k1] 5 times), k10—there are now 10 sts in brioche st and 10 sts in garter stitch.
Row 1 (WS) ([Slip 1 pwise wyif] twice), k8; ([yo, slip 1 pwise, k2tog] 5 times).
Row 2 (RS) ([Yo, slip 1 pwise, k2tog] 5 times), k10.

Place a locking ring marker on RS to avoid confusing RS and WS rows.

Rep Rows 1 and 2 until swatch measures 4", then BO on RS. Swatch should measure 4" in width.

FRONT & BACK (WORKED IN ONE PIECE TO UNDERARM)
With 1 strand of Highland and 1 strand of Alpaca 2 held together throughout, using long-tail cast-on method, CO 188 (204, 220) sts.

Set-Up Row (WS) ([Yo, slip 1 pwise, k1] 18 (20, 22) times); place marker; k22; place marker; ([yo, slip 1 pwise, k1] 36 (40, 44) times); place marker; k22; place marker; ([yo, slip 1 pwise, k1] 18 (20, 22) times).

Place a locking ring marker on RS to avoid confusing RS and WS rows.

SHORT JACKET

Every Row Thereafter ([Yo, slip 1 pwise, k2tog] 18 (20, 22) times); slip marker; k22; slip marker; ([yo, slip 1 pwise, k2tog] 36 (40, 44) times); slip marker; k22; slip marker; ([yo, slip 1 pwise, k2tog] 18 (20, 22) times).

Rep this row until piece measures 6 (7, 8¼)" from CO edge, ending with WS facing for next row.

Next Row (WS) Work pattern as set; at end of this row, place marker, divide the 2 strands and CO 15 sts using long-tail cast-on method.

Next Row (RS) ([Slip 1 pwise wyif] twice), k13; ([k1, k2tog, m1] 5 times); work pattern as set to end of row; place marker, divide the 2 strands and CO 15 sts using long-tail cast-on method.

Next Row (WS) ([Slip 1 pwise wyif] twice), k13, ([k1, k2tog, m1] 5 times); work pattern as set to last 30 sts; end k28, slip 1 pwise wyif, k1.

Next Row (RS) ([Slip 1 pwise wyif] twice), k28; ([yo, slip 1 pwise, k2tog] 13 (15, 17) times); k22; ([yo, slip 1 pwise, k2tog] 36 (40, 44) times); k22; ([yo, slip 1 pwise, k2tog] 13 (15, 17) times); k30.

Next Row (WS) ([Slip 1 pwise wyif] twice); k28; ([yo, slip 1 pwise, k2tog] 13 (15, 17) times); k22; ([yo, slip 1 pwise, k2tog] 36 (40, 44) times); k22; ([yo, slip 1 pwise, k2tog] 13 (15, 17) times); k28, slip 1 wyif, k1.

Rep these last 2 rows until there are 8 rows after the new sts were cast on.

MAKE BUTTONHOLES
Next Row (RS) K5, BO 3, k14, BO 3, k5; continue pattern as set.
Next Row (WS) Work in pattern as set to last 30 sts; k5, CO 3, k14, CO 3, k5.

SHAPE LAPEL
Next Row (Dec Row) (RS) Slip 1 pwise wyif, k1, k2tog, work sts as set to last 4 sts, k2tog, k2.

Continuing pattern as set, dec as above every 10th row until 15 sts rem on each lapel. Then continue without further shaping until piece measures 11½ (13, 14½)" from CO edge, ending with RS facing for next row.

DIVIDE FRONTS AND BACK AND BO UNDERARMS
Next Row (RS) Work right lapel and brioche sts as set; BO 22 garter sts; work back brioche sts as set; BO 22 garter sts; work left brioche sts and left lapel as set.

LEFT FRONT
Working on left front only, continue pattern as set until armhole measures 7½ (8, 8¼)", ending with RS facing for next row.

Next Row (RS) *K1, k2tog, m1; rep from * to last st; end k1.

Now work all sts in garter st for ¾". Place rem 15 lapel sts on one holder and 26 (30, 34) shoulder sts on another holder, leaving 24" of yarn. Break yarn.

RIGHT FRONT
Reattach yarn and work same as for left front.

BACK
Reattach yarn, work WS row, then continue in pattern as set until armhole measures 7½ (8, 8½)", ending with RS facing for next row.

Next Row (RS) *K1, k2tog, m1; rep from * to last st; end k1.

Now work all sts in garter st for ¾". Place sts on holder, leaving 36" of yarn. Break yarn.

JOIN SHOULDERS

Place right front shoulder sts on one needle and right back shouler sts on another holder. With RS's facing each other and WS facing you, join shoulder using 3-needle bind-off method. Join left shoulder in same manner.

CONTINUE LAPEL AND JOIN WITH BACK NECK

Place back neck sts on one needle and the 15 sts of right lapel on another needle. Continue lapel in garter st, **AND AT SAME TIME**, on all RS rows, knit next lapel st together with next back neck st. When half the back neck sts are knit together with collar sts, place the 15 collar sts on a holder. Work the left lapel in same manner; however, on RS row, begin by moving next st of neck to left hand needle so you can knit it together with lapel st.

JOIN BACK SEAM OF LAPEL

Place 15 sts of right lapel on one needle and 15 sts of left lapel on another needle. With RS's facing each other and WS facing you, join using 3-needle bind-off method.

SLEEVES

With 1 strand of Highland and 1 strand of Alpaca 2 held together throughout, CO 2 sts, with RS facing, beginning at underarm, pick up 92 (96, 100) sts evenly along armhole, CO 2 sts—96 (100, 104) sts on needle. Now work in garter st as follows:

Row 1 (WS) K1, slip 1 pwise wyif, knit to last 2 sts; slip 1 pwise wyif, k1.
Row 2 (RS) Knit.

Rep these 2 rows for 2" without shaping, then dec at beginning and end of every 8th row as follows:

Dec Row (RS) K2, k2tog, knit to last 4 sts, k2tog, k2.

When 50 sts rem on needle, work without further shaping until sleeve measures 17¾ (19, 20)". BO on next RS row.

FINISHING

Sew sleeve seams. Sew on buttons opposite buttonholes. Weave in ends. Block gently.

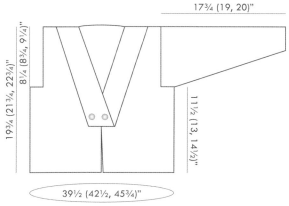

17¾ (19, 20)"

8¼ (8¾, 9¼)"

19¾ (21¾, 22¾)"

11½ (13, 14½)"

39½ (42½, 45¾)"

Textured Cap

buttery soft in baby alpaca and merino   gregory courtney

MEASUREMENTS
20½" circumference.

YARN
Isager Alpaca 2: 50 grams each of Color A and Color B. Shown in Color A, #500 (black) and Color B, #12 (green gray).

NEEDLES
16" circular US 2 (2.75 mm) and 16" circular and/or set of 5 double-pointed US 3 (3.25 mm). *Adjust needle size to obtain gauge.*

GAUGE
7 sts = 1".

CAP
With US 2 and Color A, CO 144 sts. Join, being careful not to twist and knit in the rnd as follows:

BRIM PATTERN (MULTIPLE OF 4 STS)
Foundation Rnd With Color A, *p1, k1; rep from * to end of rnd.
Rnds 1 & 2 With Color B, *p1, k1, p1, slip 1 pwise wyib; rep from * to end of rnd.
Rnds 3 & 4 With Color A, *p1, k1; rep from * to end of rnd.

Rep Rnds 1-4 until brim measures 1½" from CO edge, ending after working rnd 4 of **Brim Pattern**.

MAIN PATTERN (MULTIPLE OF 4 STS)
Rnd 1 With Color B, *p1, k1; rep from * to end of rnd.
Rnd 2 With Color B, *k1, p1; rep from * to end of rnd.
Rnd 3 With Color A, *p1, k1, p1, slip 1 pwise wyib; rep from * to end of rnd.
Rnd 4 With Color A, *k1, p1, k1, slip 1 pwise wyib; rep from * to end of rnd.

Rep Rnds 1-4 until piece measures 6" from CO edge, ending after working rnd 4 of **Main Pattern**.

DECREASE FOR CROWN
Next Rnd With Color B, *([p1, k1] 5 times), k2tog; rep from *—*132 sts rem.*
Next Rnd With Color B, *([k1, p1] 4 times), k1, p2tog; rep from * to end of rnd—*120 sts rem.*

Next Rnd With Color A, *([p1, k1, p1, slip 1 pwise wyib] twice); p1, slip 1 pwise wyib; rep from * to end of rnd.
Next Rnd With Color A, *([k1, p1, k1, slip 1 pwise wyib] twice); k1, slip 1 pwise wyib; rep from * to end of rnd.

Next Rnd With Color B, *([p1, k1] 4 times), k2tog; rep from * to end of rnd—*108 sts rem.*
Next Rnd With Color B, *([k1, p1] 3 times), k1 p2tog; rep from * to end of rnd—*96 sts rem.*

Next Rnd Work Rnd 3 of **Main Pattern**.
Next Rnd Work Rnd 4 of **Main Pattern**.

Next Rnd With Color B, *([p1, k1] 3 times), k2tog; rep from * to end of rnd—*84 sts rem.*
Next Rnd With Color B, *([k1, p1] 2 times), k1, p2tog; rep from * to end of rnd—*72 sts rem.*

At this point, change to double-pointed needles—18 sts on each of 4 needles.

Next Rnd With Color A, *p1, k1, p1, slip 1 pwise wyib, p1, slip 1 pwise wyib; rep from * to end of rnd.
Next Rnd With Color A, *k1, p1, k1, slip 1 pwise wyib, k1, slip 1 pwise wyib; rep from * to end of rnd.

Next Rnd With Color B, *([p1, k1] 2 times), k2tog; rep from * to end of rnd—*60 sts rem.*
Next Rnd With Color B, *k1, p1, k1, p2tog; rep from * to end of rnd —*48 sts rem.*

Next Rnd Work Rnd 3 of **Main Pattern**.
Next Rnd Work Rnd 4 of **Main Pattern**.

Next Rnd With Color B, *p1, k1, k2tog; rep from * to end of rnd—*36 sts rem.*
Next Rnd With Color B, *k1, p2tog; rep from * to end of rnd—*24 sts rem.*

Next Rnd With Color A, *p1, slip 1 pwise wyib; rep from * to end of rnd.
Next Rnd With Color A, *k1, slip 1 pwise wyif; rep from * to end of rnd.

Next Rnd With Color B, *k2tog; rep from * to end of rnd—*12 sts rem.*

Break yarn, leaving a 10" tail, thread onto darning needle, push through rem 12 sts, push to inside of cap and weave in. Weave in any other ends. This cap doesn't need blocking.

Buttoned Pullover

classic raglan shaping in a deep rib   beatrice smith

MEASUREMENTS
Chest 39 (42)".
Length 24 (26)".
Length to Underarm 14 (15)".
Armhole Depth 10 (11)".
Sleeve Length (underarm to cuff) 15 (15)".

YARN
450 (450) grams of Isager Alpaca 2 and 350 (350) grams of Isager Spinni/Wool 1. Shown in Alpaca 2 #16 (chartreuse) and Spinni #40 (chartreuse).

Hold 1 strand of Alpaca 2 and 1 strand of Spinni together throughout.

NEEDLES
16" and 32" circular US 5 (3.75 mm). *Adjust needle size to obtain gauge.*

NOTIONS
Stitch markers. Eight 1¾" diameter buttons.

GAUGE
31 sts and 41 rows in rib pattern on US 5 (3.75 mm).

DESIGNER NOTE
Work garment in the round from the top downwards—beginning with neck—to armholes then divide for front, back and sleeves and work back and forth in rows. Rib pattern is given first for working in rnds, then for working back and forth in rows.

NECKBAND
With 16" circular US 5, and 1 strand of Alpaca 2 and 1 strand of Spinni held together throughout, CO 120 (120) sts. Place marker for beginning of rnd and work in the rnd as follows:

Rnd 1 *P3, k1; rep from * to end of rnd.
Rnd 2 K1; *p1, k3; rep from * to last 3 sts; end p1, k2.

Rep these 2 rnds until neckband measures 6 (7)" from CO edge.

BEGIN RAGLAN SHAPING
M1, work next 35 (35) sts in rib pattern as set, m1 (**back**); place marker; work next 9 (9) sts in rib pattern as set (**left back raglan**); place marker; m1, work next 7 (7) sts in rib pattern as set, m1 (**left sleeve**); place marker; work next 9 (9) sts in rib pattern as set (**left front raglan**); place marker; m1, work next 35 (35) sts in rib pattern as set, m1 (**front**); place marker; work 9 (9) sts in rib pattern as set (**right front raglan**); place marker; m1, work 7 (7) sts in rib pattern as set, m1 (**right sleeve**); place marker; work 9 (9) sts in rib pattern as set (**right back raglan**)—*128 (128) sts on needle.*

YOKE
Continue working in rib pattern as set, **AND AT SAME TIME,** inc 1 st before and after each raglan at markers as established on every rnd 2 of rib pattern until you have worked 52 (56) inc rnds, ending after working rnd 2 of rib pattern. There will be 139 (147) sts each

BUTTONED PULLOVER

for front and back, 111 (119) sts for each sleeve and 9 (9) sts for each of the 4 raglans—536 (568 sts) on needle and raglan will measure approx 10 (11)" from beginning of raglan shaping.

DIVIDE FOR BACK, FRONT & SLEEVES
Next Rnd (Rnd 1 of Rib Pattern): Work next 139 (147) sts; work next 9 (9) raglan sts; work next 111 (119) sts and place these 111 (119) sts on holder for left sleeve.

Work next 9 (9) raglan sts; work next 139 (147) sts; work next 9 (9) raglan sts; place these 157 (165) sts on holder for front.

Work next 111 (119) sts and place on holder for right sleeve.

Work next 9 (9) raglan sts; break yarn and slide last 9 (9) sts worked back onto left-hand needle—157 (165) sts now on needle for back of garment.

CAST ON BUTTON BANDS AND WORK BACK ONLY
Next Row (RS) K2; *p1, k3; rep from * to last 3 sts; p1, k2; CO 8 sts.
Next Row (WS) *P1, k3; rep from * to last st; p1; CO 8 sts—
173 (181) sts on needle.

Now continue rib pattern as follows:

Row 1 (RS) K2; *p1, k3; rep from * to last 3 sts; end p1, k2.
Row 2 (WS) Slip 1 pwise wyif; *p1, k3; rep from * to last 3 sts; end p1, k1, slip 1 pwise wyif.

Rep these 2 rows until back measures 14 (15)" from underarm. BO in pattern.

CAST ON BUTTON BANDS AND WORK FRONT ONLY
Move 157 (165) front sts from holder to needle and work as follows:

Next Row (RS) K2; *p1, k3; rep from * to last 3 sts; p1, k2; CO 8 sts.

Next Row (WS) *P1, k3; rep from * to last st; p1; CO 8 sts—*173 (181) sts on needle.*

Now continue rib pattern as follows:

Row 1 (RS) K2; *p1, k3; rep from * to last 3 sts; end p1, k2.
Row 2 (WS) Slip 1 pwise wyif; *p1, k3; rep from * to last 3 sts; end p1, k1, slip 1 pwise wyif.

Rep these last 2 rows 5 times (10 rows in all).

Buttonhole Row 1 (RS) Work 3, BO 3, work to last 6 sts; BO 3, work 2.
Buttonhole Row 2 (WS) Slip 1 pwise wyif, work 2, CO 3, work to last 3 sts; CO 3, work 2, slip 1 pwise wyif.

Work **Rib Row 1 & 2** for 36 (36) rows.
Work **Buttonhole Row 1 & 2** to make 2nd set of buttonholes.
Work **Rib Row 1 & 2** for 36 (36) rows.
Work **Buttonhole Row 1 & 2** to make 3rd set of buttonholes.
Work **Rib Row 1 & 2** for 36 (36) rows.
Work **Buttonhole Row 1 & 2** to make 4th set of buttonholes.
Work **Rib Row 1 & 2** until same length as back, ending with RS facing for next row. BO in pattern.

SLEEVES (WORK EACH SEPARATELY)
Move 111 (119) sleeve sts from holder to needle.

Next Row (RS) K2, work in rib pattern as set to last 2 sts, k2.
Next Row (WS) P2, work in rib pattern as set to last 2 sts last 2 sts, p2.

Rep these last 2 rows until there are 10 rows.

Next Row (Dec Row) (RS) K2, ssk, work in rib pattern as set to last 4 sts, k2tog, k2.

Continue in rib pattern as set, **AND AT SAME TIME**, work **Dec Row** on every 6th (6th) row until you have decreased 19 (19) times. Continue without further shaping on rem 73 (81) sts until sleeve measures 15 (15)" from underarm, ending with RS facing for next row. BO firmly, **AND AT SAME TIME**, dec 8 (10) sts evenly spaced around.

FINISHING
Sew sleeve seams. Sew on buttons opposite buttonholes. Weave in ends. Block gently.

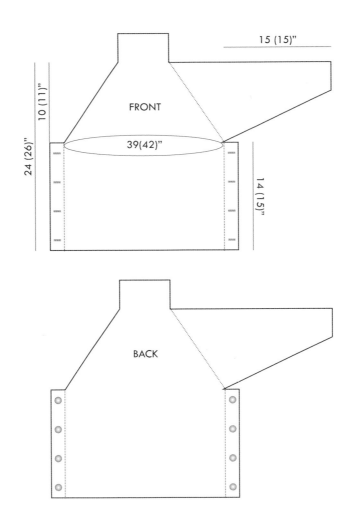

15 (15)"

10 (11)"

24 (26)"

FRONT

39(42)"

14 (15)"

BACK

Cabled Pullover

hidden shaping—a great fit in a top-down knit   marianne isager

MEASUREMENTS
Chest 41¾ (44, 46½)".
Length 21¾ (23½, 25½)".
Sleeve Length To Underarm 17¾ (18¾, 19¾)".

YARN
250 (300, 350) grams of Isager Highland.
200 (250, 250) grams of Isager Alpaca 1.

Shown in Highland Truffle and Alpaca 1 #284 (lt. natural brown).

Hold 1 strand of Highland and 1 strand of Alpaca 1 together throughout.

NEEDLES
16" and 24" circular US 3 (3.25 mm) and US 4 (3.5 mm). Set of double-pointed US 3 and US 4.
Adjust needle sizes to obtain gauge.

NOTIONS
Cable needle. Split ring stitch markers. Stitch holders or spare yarn.

GAUGE
27 sts and 29 rows = 4" in stockinette st on US 4.

2X3 RIB
Every Rnd *P2, k3; rep from * to end of rnd.

SPECIAL ABBREVIATIONS
C4F Slip 2 sts to cn and hold at front, k2; k2 from cn.
C6F Slip 3 sts to cn and hold at front, k3; k3 from cn.

C8F Slip 4 sts to cn and hold at front, k4; k4 from cn.
C10F Slip 5 sts to cn and hold at front, k5; k5 from cn.

CONSTRUCTION NOTE
Work pullover in the rnd, in one piece, from the neckband downwards.

NECKBAND
With 16" circular US 3, CO 120 (120, 120) sts using long-tail cast-on. Place split ring marker for beg of rnd and work in the rnd in garter st as follows:

Rnds 1, 3 & 5 Purl.
Rnds 2, 4 & 6 Knit.

Now work in **2X3 Rib** until neckband measures 1½ (1½, 1½)" from CO edge. In last row, place split ring marker after first 62 sts.

SHAPE FRONT NECK
Next Rnd ([P1, m1, p1, k1, m1, k2] 12 times); p1, m1, p1—87 sts between markers. Don't finish rnd— continue with short rows as follows to shape front neck—*don't include yo's made at beg of short rows in st count.*

Turn (WS) Yo, ([k1, p1, k1, p4]) 12 times), k1, p1, k1; remove marker; p3, k2; replace marker—*92 sts between markers.*

Turn (RS) Yo, p1, m1, p1, k1, m1, k2, ([p1, slip 1 pwise wyib, p1, k4] 12 times), p1, slip 1 pwise wyib, p1; remove marker (from between yo and next st); k2tog

CABLED PULLOVER

(yo and next st), m1, k2, p1, m1, p1; replace marker—
101 sts between markers.

Turn (WS) Yo, ([k1, p1, k1, p4] 14 times), k1, p1, k1;
remove marker; p2tog tbl (yo and next st), p2, k2;
replace marker—*106 sts between markers.*

Turn (RS) Yo, p1, m1, p1, k1, m1, k2, ([p1, slip 1 pwise
wyib, p1, k4] 14 times), p1, slip 1 pwise wyib, p1;
remove marker; k2tog (yo and next st), m1, k2, p1,
m1, p1; replace marker—*115 sts between markers.*

Turn (WS) Yo, ([k1, p1, k1, p4] 16 times), k1, p1, k1;
remove marker; p2tog tbl (yo and next st), p2, k2;
replace marker—*120 sts between markers.*

Turn (RS) Yo, p1, m1, p1, k1, m1, k2 ([p1, slip 1 pwise
wyib, p1, k4] 16 times), p1, slip 1 pwise wyib, p1;
remove marker; k2tog (yo and next st), m1, k2, p1,
m1, p1; replace marker—*129 sts between markers.*
Without turning, continue rnd as follows: ([k1, m1, k2,
p1, m1, p1] 5 times), k1, m1, k1, k2tog (yo and next
st)—rnd complete; place marker for beginning of
rnd—*168 sts on needle.*

YOKE
Change to 16" circular US 4 and work yoke as follows:

Rnds 1, 3, 5 & 7 *P1, k1, p1, k4; rep from *.
Rnds 2 & 6 *P1, slip 1 pwise wyib, p1, C4F; rep from
* to end of rnd.
Rnd 4 *P1, slip 1 pwise wyib, p1, k4; rep from *.
Rnd 8 (Inc Rnd) *M1, p1, slip 1 pwise wyib, p1, m1,
k4; rep from *—*216 sts on needle.*
Rnds 9, 11 & 13 *P2, k1, p2, k4; rep from *.
Rnd 10: *P2, slip 1 pwise wyib, p2, C4F; rep from *.
Rnd 12: *P2, slip 1 pwise wyib, p2, k4; rep from *.
Rnd 14 (Inc Rnd) *P2, slip 1 pwise wyib, p2; slip next
2 sts onto cn, with cn pick up bar before next st from
back to front, hold cn at front of work, with circular

needle, knit into front and back of next st, k1, k3 from
cn; rep from *—*264 sts on needle.*
Rnds 15, 17, 19, 21, 23 & 25 *P2, k1, p2, k6; rep
from *.
Rnds 16, 18, 22 & 24 *P2, slip 1 pwise wyib, p2, k6;
rep from *.
Rnd 20 *P2, slip 1 pwise wyib, p2, C6F; rep from *.
Rnd 26 (Inc Rnd) *M1, p2, slip 1 pwise wyib, p2, m1,
C6F; rep from *—*312 sts on needle.*

Change to 24" circular US 4.

Rnds 27, 29 & 31 *P3, k1, p3, k6; rep from *.
Rnds 28 & 30 *P3, slip 1 pwise wyib, p3, k6; rep
from *.
Rnd 32 (Inc Rnd) *P3, slip 1 pwise wyib, p3; slip next
3 sts onto cn, with cn pick up bar before next st from
back to front, hold cn at front of work, with circular
needle, knit into front and back of next st, k2, k4 from
cn—*360 sts on needle.*
Rnds 33, 35, 37 & 39 *P3, k1, p3, k8; rep from *.
Rnds 34, 36 & 38 *P3, slip 1 pwise wyib, p3, k8; rep
from *.
Rnd 40 (Inc Rnd) *M1, p3, slip 1 pwise wyib, p3, m1,
C8F; rep from *—*408 sts on needle.*
Rnds 41, 43, 45 & 47 *P4, k1, p4, k8; rep from *.
Rnds 42, 44 & 46 *P4, slip 1 pwise wyib, p4, k8; rep
from *.

1st Size Only
Rnd 48 *P4, slip 1 pwise wyib, p4, C8F; rep from *—
408 sts on needle.

End of yoke instructions for **1st Size Only**. Skip to
DIVIDE FRONT, BACK & SLEEVES.

2nd & 3rd Sizes Only
Rnd 48 (Inc Rnd) *P4, slip 1 pwise wyib, p4, slip next
4 sts onto cn, with cn pick up bar before next st from
back to front, hold cn at front of work, with circular

needle, knit into front and back of next st, k3, k5 from cn; rep from *—*456 sts on needle.*

Rnds 49, 51, 53, 55 & 57 *P4, k1, p4, k10; rep from *.

Rnds 50, 52, 54 & 56 *P4, slip 1 pwise wyib, p4, k10; rep from *.

Rnd 58 *P4, slip 1 pwise wyib, p4, C10F; rep from *—*456 sts on needle.*

End of yoke instructions for **2nd Size Only**. Skip to **DIVIDE FRONT, BACK & SLEEVES**.

3rd Size Only

Rnds 59, 61, 63, 65 & 67 *P4, k1, p4, k10; rep from *.

Rnds 60, 62, 64 & 66 *P4, slip 1 pwise wyib, p4, k10; rep from *.

Rnd 68 (Inc Rnd) *M1, p4, slip 1 pwise wyib, p4, m1, C10F; rep from *—*504 sts on needle.*

DIVIDE FRONT, BACK & SLEEVES
Read this section carefully before proceeding.

All Sizes: From here on, you'll work in pattern as set, slipping the st between the purl sts every other rnd, and crossing the cables on every 8th (10th, 10th) rnd.

First Rnd Remove marker; work 13 (14, 16) sts; place next 85 (95, 105) sts on holder for **left sleeve**; CO 17 (19, 21) sts; work 119 (133, 147) sts for **back**; place next 85 (95, 105) sts on holder for **right sleeve**; CO 17 (19, 21) sts; work 119 (133, 147) sts for **front**; k4 (5, 5) sts; replace marker—*you have worked 17 (19, 21) sts of the rnd twice in order to reposition the beg of rnd. There are now 272 (304, 336) sts on needle.*

Now work body sts only. There are 16 reps of pattern for body of pullover as follows:

1st Size *P4, k1, p4, k8; rep from *.
2nd Size *P4, k1, p4, k10; rep from *.
3rd Size *P5, k1, p5, k10; rep from *.

When pullover measures approx 18¾ (20, 21¾)" from shoulder, having just worked a rnd with a cable crossing, change to 24" circular US size 3 and work 3 more pattern rnds as set, then dec for waistband as follows:

1st Size *P2, k1, k2tog, k1, p2, k2tog, k2, p2, k3; rep from *—*there are 15 sts in patten rep and 240 sts on needle.*
2nd Size *P2, k1, k2tog, k1, p2, k2tog, k2, p2tog, p2tog, k3; rep from *—*there are 15 sts in pattern rep and 240 sts on needle.*
3rd Size *P2tog, p2tog, k3, p2tog, p2tog, k3, p2tog, p2tog, k3; rep from *—*there are 15 sts in pattern rep and 240 sts on needle.*

WAISTBAND
Work in **2X3 Rib** for 2 (2½, 2¾)", then knit garter edge as follows:

Rnds 1, 3 & 5 Purl.
Rnds 2 & 4 Knit.

BO in knit.

SLEEVES
Place 85 (95, 105) sts from holder onto 16" circular US 4; pick up 17 (19, 21) sts along cast-on edge at underarm, placing marker after 4th (5th, 5th) picked-up st to mark new beg of rnd—*there are 6 pattern reps and 102 (114, 126) sts on needle.*

NOTE: *Work sleeve decs on rnds where cables are crossed. Change to double-pointed needles when sts become stretched on circular needle.*

CABLED PULLOVER

1st Size Only
Continue in pattern as set, crossing cables every 8th rnd, until sleeve measures approx 5¼" from underarm—last rnd worked is rnd before cable crossing rnd.

1st Dec Rnd *P2tog, p2, slip 1 pwise wyib, p2, p2tog, C8F; rep from *—*90 sts rem.*

Continue in pattern as set until sleeve measures approx 10¼" from underarm—last rnd worked is rnd before cable crossing rnd.

2nd Dec Rnd *P3, slip 1 pwise wyib, p3, slip 4 sts onto cn, hold at front of work, k2tog, k2; ssk, k2 from cn; rep from *—*78 sts rem.*

Pattern rep is now *p3, k1 or slip 1 pwise wyib, p3, k6 or C6F; rep from *. Continue in pattern as set, crossing cables every 6th rnd, until sleeve measures 15¼" from underarm. **SKIP TO CUFF: ALL SIZES.**

2nd Size Only
Continue in pattern as set, crossing cables every 10th rnd, until sleeve measures approx 4¼" from underarm—last rnd worked is rnd before cable crossing rnd.

1st Dec Rnd *P4, slip 1 pwise wyib, p4, slip 5 sts onto cn, hold at front of work, k2 tog, k3; ssk, k3 from cn; rep from *—*102 sts rem.*

Pattern rep is now *p4, k1 or slip 1 pwise wyib, p4, k8 or C8F; rep from *.

Continue in pattern as set, crossing cables every 8th rnd, until sleeve measures approx 8¾" from underarm—last rnd worked is rnd before cable crossing rnd.

2nd Dec Rnd *P2tog, p2, slip 1 pwise wyib, p2, p2tog, C8F; rep from *—*90 sts rem.*

Pattern rep is now *P3, slip 1 pwise wyib or k1, p3, k8 or C8F; rep from *.

Continue in pattern as set until sleeve measures approx 13" from underarm—last rnd worked is rnd before cable crossing rnd.

3rd Dec Rnd: *P3, slip 1 pwise wyib, p3, slip 4 sts onto cn, hold at front of work, k2tog, k2; ssk, k2 from cn; rep from *—*78 sts rem.*

Pattern rep is now *p3, slip 1 pwise wyib or k1, p3, k6 or C6F; rep from *.

Continue in pattern as set, crossing cables every 6th rnd, until sleeve measures 16¼" from underarm. There are 13 sts in pattern rep. **SKIP TO CUFF—ALL SIZES.**

3rd Size Only
Continue in pattern as set, crossing cables every 10th rnd, until sleeve measures 3½" from underarm—last rnd worked is rnd before cable crossing rnd.

1st Dec Rnd *P5, slip 1 pwise wyib, p5, slip 5 sts onto cn, hold at front of work, k2tog, k3; ssk, k3 from cn; rep from *—*114 sts rem.*

Pattern rep is now *p5, k1 or slip 1 pwise wyib, p5, k8 or C8F; rep from *.

Continue in pattern as set, crossing cables every 8th rnd, until sleeve measures approx 7" from underarm—last rnd worked is rnd before cable crossing rnd.

2nd Dec Rnd *P2tog, p3, slip 1 pwise wyib, p3, p2tog, C8F; rep from *—*102 sts rem.*

Pattern rep is now *p4, k1 or slip 1 pwise wyib, p4, k8 or C8F; rep from *.

Continue in pattern as set until sleeve measures approx 10¾" from underarm—last rnd worked is rnd before cable crossing rnd.

3rd Dec Rnd *P2tog, p2, slip 1 pwise wyib, p2, p2tog, C8F; rep from *—*90 sts rem.*

Pattern rep is now *p3, k1 or slip 1 pwise wyib, p3, k8 or C8F; rep from *.

Continue in pattern as set until sleeve measures approx 14¼" from underarm—last rnd worked is rnd before cable crossing rnd.

4th Dec Rnd *P2tog, p1, slip 1 pwise wyib, p1, p2tog, C8F; rep from *—*78 sts rem.*

Pattern rep is now *p2, k1 or slip 1 pwise wyib, p2, k8 or C8F; rep from *.

Continue in pattern as set until sleeve measures 17¼" from underarm.

CUFF—ALL SIZES
Change to double-pointed US 3.

Next Rnd *K2tog, k1, k2tog, p2, k1, k2tog, k1, p2; rep from *—60 (60, 60) sts rem.

Next Rnd *K3, p2; rep from *.

Rep this rnd until cuff measures 2 (2, 2)", then knit garter edge as follows:

Rnds 1, 3 & 5 Purl.
Rnds 2 & 4 Knit.

BO in knit.

FINISHING
Weave in ends. Block gently.

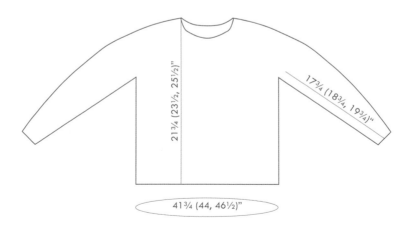

41¾ (44, 46½)"

21¾ (23½, 25½)"

17¾ (18¾, 19¾)"

Rendemaske Scarf

feather weight fabric in the running stitch

marianne isager

MEASUREMENTS
Width 18".
Length 70".

This scarf tends to grow in both width and length after washing/blocking and with wear. To knit a narrower or wider scarf, the st pattern is a multiple of 7 sts + 6 sts.

YARN
Color A 100 grams of Isager Highland or Tvinni.
Color B 100 grams of Isager Highland or Tvinni.
Color C 50 grams of Isager Alpaca 2.

Colorway 1 shown opposite in Color A, Tvinni #30 (black); Color B, Highland Oxford; and Color C, Alpaca 2 #16 (chartreuse).
Colorway 2 shown on pages 2-3 in Color A, Highland Maize; Color B, Tvinni #13 (pale sage); and Color C, Alpaca 2 #100 (natural white).
Colorway 3 shown on page 96 in Color A, Highland Tobacco; Color B, Highland Scots Pine; and Color C, Alpaca 2 #25 (red).

NEEDLES
Straight or circular US 4 (3.5 mm). *Adjust needle size to obtain gauge.*

GAUGE
23 sts = 4" in garter st on US 4.

NOTES *Near the end of this scarf, you'll be dropping the stitches made by the yo's from their point of origin all the way down the scarf to near the bottom. If your st count should change because of accidental increases or decreases, these may not drop all the way down the scarf. To keep track,*

*run a thread of scrap yarn up your work to mark
these stitches. Don't weave ends into the stitch made
by the yo, as it will be difficult to drop.*

SCARF
With Color A, CO 104 sts.

Rows 1-12 With Color A, knit.
Row 13 With Color C, k6; *yo, k2tog, k5; rep to
end of row.
Row 14 With Color C, knit.

Now continue in garter st (knit every row)—
breaking off and reattaching colors as
needed—as follows:

*With Color B, knit 12 rows (6 garter ridges).
With Color C, knit 2 rows (1 garter ridge).
With Color A, knit 12 rows (6 garter ridges).

With Color C, knit 2 rows (1 garter ridge).

Rep from * until scarf measures approx 68",
ending after working 12 rows of Color B.

Next Row With Color C, *k6, drop next stitch;
rep from * to last 6 sts; end k6.
Next Row With Color C, knit.

With Color A, knit 12 rows.

With Color A, BO in knit. With a crochet hook or
short needle, continue dropping sts down through
scarf to their point of origin (they won't drop any
further).

FINISHING
Weave in ends. Gently hand wash or steam
lightly to even out and open up dropped stitches.

18"

70"

Black and White Jacket

graphical style in bold stripes   carol lapin

MEASUREMENTS
Chest 40 (43½, 47)".
Length to Back of Neck 24 (24¾, 25½)".
Sleeve Length 19 (19½, 20)".

YARN
Color A 200 (250, 250) grams of Isager Tvinni #0 (natural white).
Color B 250 (300, 300) grams of Isager Alpaca 2 #500 (black).

NEEDLES
Short US 3 (3.25 mm) for panels. Two 24" circular US 3 to join panels and sleeves. Two 60" circular US 3 to join lapel to jacket. *Adjust needle size to obtain gauge.*

NOTIONS
One large button. Stitch holders or spare yarn.

GAUGE
25 sts and 56 rows = 4" in garter st on US 3 (3.25 mm).

CONSTRUCTION NOTES
Work jacket body in panels and join together using 3-needle bind-off method. Join sleeves and lapel to body in same manner.

PANEL A (Center Back)—make 1
With Color A, CO 40 (42, 44) sts and knit 10 rows.

Decrease Row K1, k2tog, k to last 3 sts, k2tog, k1—38 (40, 42) sts rem.

Change to Color B and knit 11 rows. On 12th row, work **Decrease Row** as given above—36 (38, 40) sts rem.

Change to Color A and knit 11 rows. On 12th row, work **Decrease Row** as given above—34 (36, 38) sts rem.

Continue as set, alternating 12 rows (6 garter ridges) of Color A and 12 rows (6 garter ridges) of Color B, working **Decrease Row** on 12th row of each stripe, until 20 (22, 24) sts rem.

Now continue as set, alternating 12 rows of Color A and 12 rows of Color B, *without decreasing*, until there are 28 (29, 30) stripes from CO edge. Knit 6 rows (3 garter ridges) in color as for next stripe and place 20 (22, 24) rem sts on holder.

PANEL B—make 4
With Color A, CO 40 (42, 44) sts and knit 1 row.
With Color B, knit 2 rows.
With Color A, knit 2 rows.
With Color B, knit 2 rows.
With Color A, knit 2 rows.
With Color B, knit 1 row.

Decrease Row With Color B, k1, k2tog, k to last 3 sts, k2tog, k1—38 (40, 42) sts rem.

Continue as set, alternating 2 rows of Color A and 2 rows of Color B, working **Decrease Row** on 12th row (Color B), until 20 (22, 24) sts rem.

Now continue as set, alternating 2 rows of Color A and 2 rows of Color B, until there are 348 (360, 372) rows—174 (180, 186) garter ridges—from CO edge. Place sts on holder. *Note—cast-on and first row (Color A) count as 1st garter ridge.*

PANEL C—MAKE 4
Work as for **Panel A**, until there are of 29 (30, 31) stripes. Place sts on holders.

PANEL D (UNDERARM)—MAKE 2
With Color A, CO 46 (48, 50) sts. Work exactly as for **Panel B**, dec'g until 24 (26, 28) sts rem. Now continue in stripe sequence as set, **without dec'g**, until there are 224 (230, 236) rows—112 (115, 118) garter ridges—from CO edge. BO. *Note—cast-on and first row (Color A) count as 1st garter ridge.*

SLEEVES—MAKE 2
With Color B, CO 63 (63, 63) sts, and beginning with WS, work in stockinette st for 25 rows.

Next Row (RS) K7, m1, ([k10, m1] 5 times), k6—69 (69, 69) *sts on needle.*
Next Row (WS) Knit to form fold line for hem.

Now, beginning with RS, work checkerboard pattern as follows, repeating the 8 pattern rows 3 times for a total of 24 rows and 6 "checkerboards":

Rows 1 & 3 *K3B, k3A; rep from * to last 3 sts; k3B.

Rows 2 & 4 *P3B, p3A; rep from * to last 3 sts; p3B.
Rows 5 & 7 *K3A, k3B; rep from * to last 3 sts; k3A.
Rows 6 & 8 *P3A, p3B; rep from * to last 3 sts; p3A.

Next Row (RS) With Color B, inc as follows:

1st Size K11, m1, ([k23, m1] 2 times), k12—*72 sts on needle.*
2nd Size K8, m1, ([k13, m1] 4 times), k9—*74 sts on needle.*
3rd Size K7, m1, ([k9, m1] 6 times), k8—*76 sts on needle.*

Next Row (WS) With Color B, knit.

Change to Color A, and working in garter stitch as for **Panel B**— alternating 2 rows of Color A and 2 rows of Color B—work sleeve, **AND AT SAME TIME**, inc 1 st at beginning and end of every 6th row 2 (5, 12) times, then every 8th row 20 (18, 14) times. Continue as set without shaping on rem 116 (120, 128) sts until sleeve measures 19 (19½, 20)" from checkerboard cuff edge (do not include cuff lining in measurement) ending after working 2 rows of Color B. Leave sts on needle.

JOIN PANELS AND SHOULDERS
With separate 24" circular needles, RS facing and Color B, pick up an equal number of sts evenly along panel edges—*as a general rule, pick up 1 st in each garter ridge*—and join panels A, B,

BLACK AND WHITE JACKET

C, and D using 3-needle bind-off method—**see schematic for panel arrangement**. Place shoulder sts onto US 3 needles and join using 3-needle bind-off method.

LAPEL

With US 3 and Color B, CO 45 (45, 45) sts.

Rows 1 & 3 (RS) K20B, p1B, ([k3A, k3B] 4 times).
Rows 2 & 4 ([P3B, k3A] 4 times), k1B, p20B.

These 4 rows form the lapel—solid black is hem, folded under—black and white checkerboard is outer lapel—and the single black stitch is the turn row.

Continue these 4 rows until lapel measures 12½ (12½, 12½)", ending with RS facing for next row.

MAKE BUTTONHOLE

Next Row (RS) K5B, BO 9 sts, k6B, p1B, k3A, k3B, k3A, BO 9 sts, k3A, k3B.
Next Row (WS) P3B, p3A, CO 9 sts, p3A, p3B, p3A, k1B, p6B, CO 9 sts, p5B.

Continue as set until lapel measures approximately 52½ (53¼, 54)" from CO edge. *As tensions vary slightly, it is important that the lapel fits along right front edge of jacket, then around back neck, then along left front edge when slightly stretched. Length should be adjusted in rows of 4 to make a complete checkerboard at the end.* With Color B, bind off.

JOIN LAPEL TO JACKET

With 60" circular needle, RS facing and Color B, pick up approx 45 (48, 51) sts along first half of right front of jacket, 45 (48, 51) sts along 2nd half of right front, 20 (22, 24) sts along back neck, 45 (48, 51) sts along first half of left front and 45 (48, 51) sts along 2nd half of left front—approx 200 (214, 228) sts in all. With another 60" circular needle, RS facing and Color

B, pick up the same number of sts along lapel. Join lapel to jacket using 3-needle bind-off method.

Notes—You must pick up exactly the same number of sts along the full lapel edge as you do along the right front, back neck and left front of jacket combined. Unlike sewing up a piece, any fudging for good fit must be accomplished while picking up sts.

Helpful Hint—Mark the pieces with matching pins, and be careful to pick up the same number of sts for each section on each piece. The numbers given above are a good estimate; however, yours may vary.

Tack lapel lining to inside and gently steam to give smooth finish to lapel and shape to back neck.

ATTACH SLEEVES

With 24" circular needle, RS facing and Color B, pick up 116, (120, 128) sts evenly around armhole edge. Place sts of sleeve onto another 24" circular needle. Join sleeve to armhole using 3-needle bind-off method. Rep for other sleeve.

Note—Sleeve is smaller than sleeve opening and is slightly stretched when knit together with opening to give proper fit and to avoid puckering; therefore, pick up fewer than 1 st in each garter ridge and fewer than every st at underarm.

FINISH SLEEVES

Turn cuff lining to inside and sew down. With separate 24" circular needles, RS facing and Color B, pick up an equal number of sts along each sleeve edge, omitting cuff. Join sleeve seam using 3-needle bind-off method. With Color B, sew cuff seam. Rep for other sleeve.

Darn in ends, gently press all seams, sew button to lapel opposite button hole.

Marion Foale & Ali MacGraw

Crossing Paths

DAVID CODLING

Ali MacGraw and Marion Foale—actress and fashion designer—an ocean and worlds apart and, until last year, two women I knew only by popular reputation. By happy coincidence, I've now had the pleasure of getting to know both of these seriously accomplished women who have achieved iconic status. I discovered that their seemingly diverse lives share incredible common threads (not knitting, though! Ali doesn't knit a stitch and Marion taught herself to knit for her second fashion career).

Surely they must know each other from their heady roles in the hip fashion frenzy of the 60's—at the same time that Marion was one of the trendiest fashion designers on Carnaby Street, Ali was modeling, assisting Diana Vreeland at Harper's Bazaar, and honing her skills as a top notch photo stylist. Though they share many mutual friends and associates, to my surprise, their paths had never crossed.

My partner and I first met Ali when she visited our store in Santa Fe on a button quest. Being knitters, we could hardly avoid the obvious: "What was the origin of the famous "Love Story" cap"? For cinema buffs, here's a bit of trivia—it was freezing cold during a morning shoot in New York City and taking matters into her own hands, Ali spotted a street vendor and ran to buy the hat. The rest is history—fashion *and* movie history. A project involving Ali MacGraw and knitted caps was too intriguing not to pursue and Ali agreed. Noted for her animal advocacy, we created a project that would involve "the cap" and also benefit the Wildlife Emergency Response Fund.

Only months before, I had met noted British designer Marion Foale and was working with her to bring her yarns and designs to the USA. It seemed a perfect match. Marion was excited to join our effort and to design the cap for such a worthy cause. I was still fascinated by the parallels in the lives and careers of these two women. Their paths *needed* to cross and I was excited when we all agreed to meet at Marion's studio in the English Midlands. A month later we were off . . .

Upon arrival in England, we went to Abbey Farm to scout locations for the next day's photo shoot. Marion joined us and it was obvious that my intuition about these two women was spot on! Their immediate connection was unmistakable. Listening to them sharing endless tales and laughter over the next few days, I eagerly anticipated our more directed interview planned for our last day. I'd like to share some of it with you. Though our conversation seemed to be over in minutes, we actually talked for nearly three hours. It has been edited here for time and space constraints.

Ali MacGraw & Marion Foale
Atherstone, September 2010

David *You both have spent a great part of your lives in the public eye. How would you say others define you?*

Ali It's always a preconception based on what I used to do for a living: an attendant, often inaccurate, sometimes gushy, warped celebrity hit.

Marion I think they realize that I'm just about the oldest person still working in the fashion industry after all these years and I think they're just very surprised and amazed that the old bird is still kicking.

D *And your self-definition?*

M Somebody who absolutely loves to work. Somebody who cannot sit still unless it's time to go to sleep. I have to be doing something or have a project, and if I've got nothing going, I'll paint. No spaces for sitting around. The odd good film and I read.

A I'm super aware right now. There are periods of my life when I feel change, and I'm in change right now. I'm not sure where I'm going, but I've been very, very controlled all my life, even fearful. I'm in a sort of free-fall. Having gotten to this shocking age, I realize there's no more time to screw around.

M Exactly.

A . . . what do I want to eat, who is worth having supper with, which book can I not live without reading, what country haven't I seen. I just pray daily for the strength to act on that gut intuition that I've got to let it rip now because time's running out.

M Yes. Time is getting short and I feel that, too. I'm going through a change as well. I've started the yarn and knitting pattern program with David. I've wanted to do this for a long time. Behind me you see hundreds and hundreds of designs and patterns, and I cannot bear to think that I'll pop off before we've arranged them nicely for all the knitters in the world to have. This is my new project. And, along with painting, I'm still doing what I've always done.

D *Growing up, did you both discover your life's passion at an early age?*

M Ah. . . what I wanted to do when I was young? I was just absolutely a hundred percent positive that I was going to be a famous artist and that was it. Straight to art school, going to be a famous artist, and then I realized I'd have to teach and I didn't want to do teaching, so I went into fashion and I knew it was right for me because it was easy to do. I had training with my parents. They were both in the rag trade and it just fell into place. I wanted to do all things, like getting married, growing organic food, having children, educating them myself

completely. I wanted to do everything—travel, gardening, the lot.

D *And have you done everything?*

M I haven't finished. I've got a lot to do.

A I started working just to pay my way at age 14 or 15. This isn't a Dickensian story. It's just called: I needed money for school books. My parents were artists and everything that made me happy involved using their toys. "If you're bored, go out and take the pastels and draw the chickens, or go find leaves in the woods and we'll make a book out of them." I had this extraordinary influence in my house. It was not about money. It was about having a rich imagination. I didn't know what I wanted to do with that. In college I was an art history major to get credit for studio time. The art history has made my life richer. I knew that I wanted to be in that world—that whatever I did had to be in art. I was as shocked as the next person to be asked to be in a movie that turned out to be a success. It was a complete stunning shock, and that I survived it is the single biggest accomplishment in my life.

M Ah, but it wasn't only a love story. It was a magic story.

A Thank you. Still that fast track was somebody else's dream. I had very sound parents who didn't think it was

the most astonishing thing that could ever happen. In fact, they were scared. Having survived it, grateful for the goodies it gave me, I'm under no illusion that it was a healthy lifestyle for me. The universe has corroborated this because I haven't been in it for ten years and I've lived very richly, I should say, ever since.

D *Marion, you and Sally Tuffin had your "Love Story" moment of sudden fame. . .*

M Yes, when we went to the States and did whistle stop tours, the London bus and the whole explosion, it was almost scary because it was so big and so sudden.

A And I saw it. It was huge. Most of the people I knew were crazy about fashion. None of us could afford it, but we looked at the magazines. And when they came to town, we chucked

everything we owned. It's true. Everybody lucky enough to be in their 20's, in particular, hoped to imitate what you all were doing. I was working as a photo stylist at the time, so it was my job to know. It was fabulous, oh my God, to get out of those damn dirndl skirts.

M And, hey, look, they're back in!

A Wait a second. There was one other piece of equipment that we got out of that year and that was the panty girdle!

D *You've both put yourself out, however unwittingly, for public consumption. How do you deal with that?*

M Well, every time I do a collection I'm being judged, and I tell you, it terrifies me still. I'm putting myself on show, what I do. Is it good enough? Terrifying . . .

A I had a lucky first movie with amazingly supportive people and I had gotten stunningly surprising great reviews. Then comes, "how are you going to equal that one?" My self-awareness and involvement became crippling. I've learned late that, in any art, it's "do the thing." The joy and the

experience is the doing, not the "what do they think? What do they think?". Somebody's always going to think something stupid, over the top or terribly cruel. It cost me. There's only so much energy. My energy leaked to, "How's that? How do you like me? Is that okay?". It taps the energy from the place that gives the joy.

M That's right. It takes away your energy and your joy. I just enjoy coming in when it's all quiet and nothing much is happening and starting a new collection. I mean that's nice, because nobody's judging me. I'm doing what I want to do. And I will do what I want to do, even if they say that it's not in at the moment. Too bad. I'm doing it.

D *The judgment has to be somewhat different for the two of you. Marion, you're putting out a product . . .*

M I am. And it's got to keep a lot of people in business for the next six months.

D *Ali, these days, you're really putting yourself out, not so much for artistic judgment, but for more about who you are as a person . . .*

A You know, I do work occasionally. A few years ago, I was asked to do a role in a Broadway play, something I had never done in my life. It was paralyzingly frightening. I looked at the script and said, "no thank you." My son said, "Mom, you have to do this, you have to do it." In the process of getting through the fear, which was the biggest fear I think I've ever had in my life, there was a lesson in it. So I did put myself in an unnecessarily horrific place. That's a healthy change. Ok, I'm scared, but I'm going to do it anyway.

M So how did the play on Broadway go?

A It didn't! But the experience was just triumphant. Not in terms of reviews, but that I learned such respect for the work and for everybody I worked with. And, I finally wasn't an embarrassment. And that's not being coy. It's the truth. Sometimes we don't know the reasons why we are given jobs.

M Yes . . . challenges.

A Challenges. A much better word. It's exciting. Roll up your sleeves. I think at this point in our lives, you and I get to say, "Let's take a shot at that with all we've got." If it doesn't work, and we certainly know from looking at the arc of our lives that not everything works, we survive.

M In life, there are loads of ups and loads of downs and they all teach you something.

D *In an interesting way, I perceive the two of you as a combo of Yin and Yang: Marion more into doing than being and Ali more into being than doing. You both have a joie de vivre, which is enviable by any standards. How does my perception strike you?*

M Yes. I'm certainly a doer.

A The funny thing is that the "being" is a big deal. We are having that *joie de vivre* moment and soon won't. I'm not one to sit and quietly wait for something great to happen. I mean, if the day is only going to be about tea and cookies in the back room and seeing your collection, it's a major day in my life. This is an astounding little trip. Other people might say, "Oh, I have to go to England for a few days." For me, every second of it is about being alive. And that's what's left for me. The odds that someone is going to say, "There's this astonishing part and you can work for blah, blah, blah . . ." It's not going to happen and it doesn't define whether I'm alive. I am alive. So being isn't a presentation. It's real.

D *Ali, I read an interview in which you were asked to comment on the surprise success of "Love Story". You said, "If you're a baby about the media, as I was, you can't imagine what it's like when the great approval machine shines its beam on you, when every time you cross the street, someone comes out of a manhole to talk about your hair-*

cut. I have since learned that surviving stardom depends on doing the work to find out who you are so that you don't define yourself by what people say about you, but nothing can prepare you for that kind of avalanche. The mistake is to take it for the end of the story." It's fascinating that you both had massive success at a very young age and now have completely different and still very successful lives. Clearly, your early successes were not, as you say, the end of the story.

A I think it's a terrific quote. I hope I said it! I think it's the absolute truth. It's just a freak thing. The fairy godmother flicks that diamond dust at you for God knows what reason. Mine was probably my haircut. But, you know, I feel that being real is the big, big, big, thing. When you get what I got, celebrity unexpectedly at an early age, and not for something I was good at—I was good at the job before that—it's hard not to define every breath as, "What do people think?" There's no authenticity behind that. I strive at this time of my life to be real and reaction be damned. Not rude, not aggressively nasty to people, but real to the best of my ability. And I just suspect from getting to know you, Marion, over these last few days that your struggle hasn't been what mine has been, that you've been real longer than I have been?

M I don't know about that at all. Nobody can gauge how long we've

all been real because, gosh, there's that lovely story about the Velveteen Rabbit that became real. As regards all of that, I don't listen to what people say about me at all. I only judge what I do myself. And if it's not good enough for me, then it's not good enough. I judge myself and it has nothing to do with "out there."

A I didn't read my reviews at a certain point. One time some work that had meant a lot to me was just eviscerated. That day I realized that as bad as reviews are, they're not the truth. As good as they are, they're not the truth. I don't read the muck at all. And I totally agree with you: I, too, am my own best judge.

M Praise can be wonderful at the time, elating and wonderful, but then you think, hang on a minute, this isn't real, this is not you. You're going to go back home and sit in your home and make some dinner. That's you. Feed the cat, get the children to bed, I mean, that's me. I always have a laugh when magazines and such want to come in and do this thing about Marion Foale, and I often say, "Who is this Marion Foale? I don't think I've ever met her. Where is she? Where is she?"

A Hopefully, the story is a daily story right up until the great beyond. Which will be proceeded by a large amount of chocolate, many creatures sitting around, flowers . . .

D *Marion, in one of your interviews you said: "Make sure you do what you want to do. Don't get stuck in a job through your life you don't really like." I think you've been lucky . . .*

M I'm very lucky. I never worked for anybody in my life. My parents taught me to make clothes and make patterns and whatnot, so I always had that skill. I've made everything: curtains, cushion covers, bed covers, everything. My parents gave me the skill, but weren't into art in the way I was always into art. And I'm really lucky because my knitwear collections have been successful for almost 30 years now. I really love the challenge daily, getting that pattern correct. When David called and said he didn't find any mathematical faults, that was the best thing for ages! I was boasting about it. I went home and said to my daughter Polly, "Guess what? All my math was correct." I love math, love it.

A Now there's something different about us!

D *Ali, do you feel that you ever got stuck in a job you didn't like?*

A Here's a very sad story. I don't think I found my soul job. I don't think it's luck. Marion, you had the gut wisdom to realize that you were doing something you adored and that you could make work. When it became enormous, well, that might have been luck, but the fact is, whether it was up or down, you passionately did something. I didn't.

M But you are now, aren't you?

A Well, yes, but that's a lot of time. I'm not saying I wish I had never done what I did—it brought me many other adventures.

M Yes, it took you on your life's path.

A Exactly. There's no point to ever have a regret about anything. We co-created every moment that we live. I have sabotaged a lot of things. And now sitting at your design table like this . . . I would have been very happy in this room. I just didn't pick my soul work, and that's too bad.

M Do you know what your soul work is?

A I don't know it focusedly. I know that everything that gives me pleasure involves my hands and my eyes. It's the one area where I don't care and never have cared what anybody thought of it. It's funny, my mother was an astonishing woman who could do everything with about two beans to rub together. I remember her saying when I was about 8 years old, "I hope you find something to do when you're older that does not involve the approval of others because, ultimately, you're alone." She didn't mean "boo-hoo" alone, she meant that the

feed-in of other people cannot create how you feel about yourself.

M Gosh, that's an amazing memory to have all these decades later.

A She was dead right. Imagine all of our shock when after working for 15 years—gift shop, maid, waitress, photo stylist, the things we all did—I got the big American job that depends on the approval of others! My parents were horrified.

M It must have been quite frightening for them.

A It was terrifying for them. They didn't understand it at the time and they did constant checks to see if I had bought the Kool-Aid. Thank God I had parents like that, as opposed to some of these poor kids who have the stage mommy. I think to survive the entertainment business these days is just a bloody miracle. And now, to be with all of you in this beautiful village, in this incredible architecture with these flowers and animals, watching you work with paper and pen, painting when you have time . . .

M I always say I'm a really lucky person. Obviously, I've had terrible downs like everybody else.

A Life.

M Yes, personal life. It builds you into a better person, eventually.

D *It's fair to say that you both qualify for senior bus fares, but at the same time it can't be said that you lead any lesser lives for it . . .*

A There's a kind of disrespect for much older people. We're not this desirable chunk of creation that's called the perfect-looking 30-year-old. That's bullshit.

M The older generation can give us so much.

A It amazingly plays out, to circle back around, in fashion. Very, very young creatures who are divine to look at (and we all were once), are the model. I was thinking, looking at your new collection, there is one beautiful thing after another which will look one way when somebody 19 is lucky enough to wear it, but it's also going to look great on us.

M I design around all sorts of shapes and sizes of women. I never forget the big lady. I always look after her because she suffers in fashion and that's not fair. And I always think about that very tiny lady that likes to look immaculate and has got a wonderful figure—she buys lots of clothes. I don't leave anybody out. There's the pregnant lady to think about. I mean most of us were pregnant quite a bit!

A Yes, and we all need to feel great. And we have to offer respect. There's wisdom. It's the life experiences. I have to laugh—once in a while I say to my son, "You know, I've got some big news for you. I'm now old enough to tell you that I actually do know some stuff. I didn't know anything until five minutes ago, but you might want to have a listen because I did that and I can tell you how it's going to turn out." But you know what, I'm sure that my dear parents tried to say this same thing. I remember daddy said something once about some choice in men that I made—none of them that are on the pop biography—and I remember saying to him, "You don't know anything about love." Can you imagine?

M Can you imagine that? That's incredible.

A So I love the idea that we get to honor each generation not as a slide down, but as people who have something delicious going on. I have three good friends who are now in their mid-80's and, you know what, I love to see them. They still can be talked to about every single thing I can think of: sex, adventures, anything. The door doesn't close on dialogue with people who are willing to be real. It's exciting. It gives me a model for what's up ahead.

D *I don't know where the afternoon has gone, but I think it must be time for our cookies and tea?*

M It's been huge fun. Have you got any more goodies for us?

D *Maybe one more. Knitters will be sharing our chat. Is there anything you would like to say to them?*

M Well, happy knitting. I think it's the best thing to say.

A I was going to say a version of that, but, as usual, it's more long-winded! I read a book a long time ago about a young man who was killed in Somalia. He was a Reuter's photographer and his mother put together this book of his extraordinary images. The book is called, **The Journey is the Destination**. It made a profound impression on me. So I say: if you're lucky enough to know how to knit and you're making something beautiful and you have Marion as your model and icon, do it! Be thrilled with the process of doing it, love the person you give it to, realize that a piece of your treasured life is involved in the making. There's no richer way to live.

We had our farewell breakfast the next morning. In a proper English mist, we put Ali on the train to visit old friends in Wales. Marion drove back to her studio to work on her Spring collection. I headed for Heathrow and the flight home, still fascinated by these two women who have led, and continue to lead, such remarkable lives.

Marion's first hand knitting collection in nearly 25 years has now been published. You can find the **Marion Foale Collection—Book 1**, along with her signature yarn, at fine yarn stores in the United States. She continues to produce her seasonal knitwear collections for some of the finest stores in the world. And when escape from the studio is possible, you might find her most anywhere in the world on one of her painting vacations.

I remember asking Ali if she had ever knitted, and she replied, "Yes. One time in school there was a class knitting project and I worked away until it was discovered that I could only knit parallelograms". We're working on her. She ventured to *Stitches West* with us this past winter to help promote the *Ali's Cap Project* for the **Wildlife Emergency Response Fund**. I caught her talking about "finishing" and "stashes" with knitters . . . hmmm . . . "talking the talk." We never give up. Ali may yet "walk the walk"!

Ali's Cap Project

The **Wildlife Emergency Response Fund** offers immediate help whenever crisis strikes wildlife anywhere in the world. Join Marion and Ali in this worthy cause. To order your cap kit, visit www.tuttosantafe.com.

Facing Page — Ali models the cap at Abbey Farm

Lucy Wrap

easy to knit lace with a pretty ruffled edge   marion foale

MEASUREMENTS
Approx 30½" wide x 80" long.

YARN
900 grams of Marion Foale 3-Ply Wool. Shown in color 004 (cream).

NEEDLES
32" circular US 6 (4 mm). US 8 (5 mm) for binding off.

WRAP
With US 6, CO 208 sts and knit 8 rows (garter st).

Now continue in pattern with fluted edge as follows:

Row 1 (RS) K4, ([k2tog] twice), *([yo, k1] 4 times), ([k2tog] 4 times); rep from * 13 more times (14 reps in all); end ([yo, k1] 4 times), ([k2tog] twice), k24.
Row 2 K24, turn.
Row 3 Knit the 24 sts.
Row 4 Knit the 24 sts, then all rem sts—*208 sts.*
Row 5 Knit all 208 sts.
Row 6 Rep Row 2.
Row 7 Rep Row 3.
Row 8 Rep Row 4.

Rep rows 1-8 until wrap measures 80", ending after working row 1 of pattern. Knit 7 rows (garter st).

With US 8, BO in k1, p1 rib.

FINISHING
Weave in ends. Block gently.

Pattern excerpted from Marion Foale Knitting and published here with the permission of Unicorn Books and Crafts, Inc.

Ali models Marion's Lucy Wrap at Abbey Farm.

GRACE ANNA FARROW

Bump Stole

sophisticated style in bobbled rib   grace anna farrow

MEASUREMENTS
Width 21".
Length 70".

YARN
250 grams of Isager Spinni/Wool 1. Shown in #10s (lt. blue-green). Smooth scrap yarn for provisional cast-on.

NEEDLES
24" circular US 4 (3.5 mm). *Adjust needle size to obtain gauge.*

GAUGE
24 sts = 4" in pattern on US 4.

NOTE
The 3 knit sts at the beginning of every row and the 3 slipped sts at the end of every row form an i-cord edge.

STOLE
I-Cord Cast-On
1 With scrap yarn, provisionally CO 3 sts.
2 With Spinni, work 122 rows of i-cord as follows: *k3; without turning, slide sts to opposite end of needle; bring yarn from behind, tugging gently; rep from *.
3 Leaving 3 sts on needle, with RS facing, pick up 121 sts along knitted cord. Bring yarn forward between the needles. Unwork provisional cast on and slip these 3 sts onto right-hand needle, twisting them around so they appear to be purl sts—*127 sts on needle*. Don't work these last 3 sts. Turn and work charts as follows:

Reading odd-numbered (RS) rows from right to left and even-numbered (WS) rows from left to right, work Rows 1-39 rows of **Chart A** once, then rep Rows 40-63 of **Chart B** 25 times, then work Rows 64-101 of **Chart C** once. Leave sts on needle.

I-Cord Cast-Off
Next Row (WS) K3; slip these 3 sts back to left-hand needle; k3; slip these 3 sts back to left hand needle; *K2, ssk; without turning, slide sts to opposite end of needle; bring yarn from behind, tugging gently; rep from * until 3 sts rem; k3. Graft these 3 sts together with i-cord at corner.

FINISHING
Weave in ends. Block gently.

Chart A

Chart B

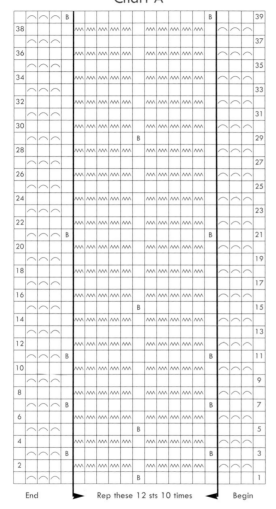

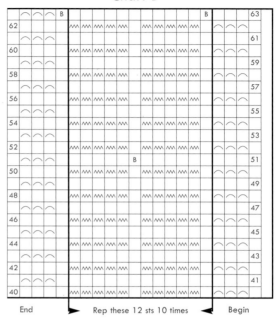

Rep rows 40-63 25 times

End → Rep these 12 sts 10 times ← Begin

End → Rep these 12 sts 10 times ← Begin

	knit on RS rows; purl on WS rows.
⌒	slip wyif.
∿	knit on WS rows.
B	make bobble: k1, yo, k1, yo, k1 in same st; turn; p5; turn; slip 3 sts tog as if to knit; k2tog; pass the 3 slipped sts over the 2 sts knitted tog.

Chart C

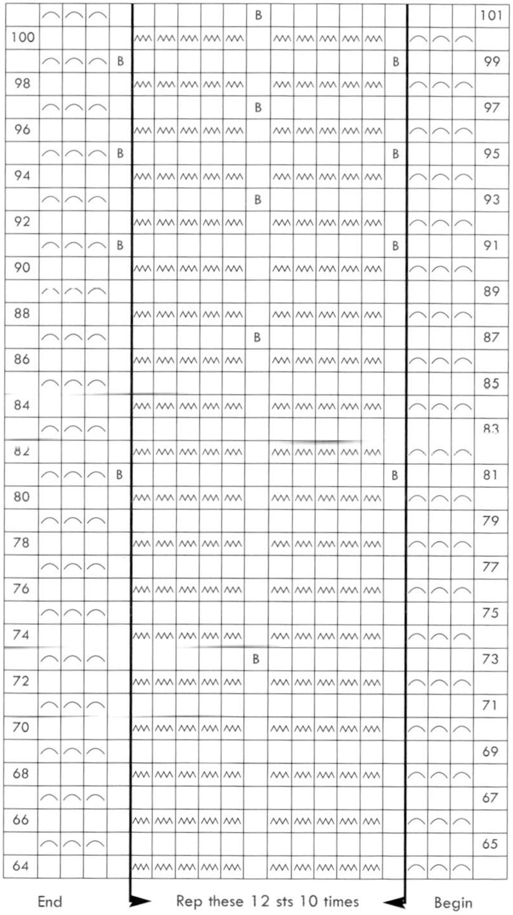

End — Rep these 12 sts 10 times — Begin

21"

70"

☐   knit on RS rows; purl on WS rows.

⌒   slip wyif.

〰   knit on WS rows.

B   make bobble: k1, yo, k1, yo, k1 in same st; turn;
p5; turn; slip 3 sts tog as if to knit; k2tog;
pass the 3 slipped sts over the 2 sts knitted tog.

TUTTO *a mano*   61

Bump Scarf

bobbles and ribs in a triangular shape   grace anna farrow

MEASUREMENTS
Width 46" at widest point.
Length 23".

YARN
150 grams of Isager Spinni/Wool 1. Shown in #4s (charcoal gray). Smooth scrap yarn for provisional cast-on.

NEEDLES
24" circular US 4 (3.5 mm). *Adjust needle size to obtain gauge.*

GAUGE
24 sts = 4" in pattern on US 4.

NOTES
1 As you work, scarf grows from 11 sts at center of flat bottom of triangle (see schematic) towards the other two flat edges with center st going upwards towards point at top of triangle.
2 The 3 knit sts at the beginning of every row and the 3 slipped sts at the end of every row form an i-cord edge.

SPECIAL ABBREVIATION
MB (make bobble) k1, yo, k1, yo, k1 in same st; turn; p5; turn; slip 3 sts tog as if to knit; k2tog; pass the 3 slipped sts over the 2 sts knitted tog.

SCARF
I-Cord Cast-On
1 Using scrap yarn, provisionally CO 4 sts.
2 With Spinni, work 4 rows of i-cord as follows: *k4; without turning, slide sts to opposite end of needle; bring yarn from behind, tugging gently; rep from *.
3 Leaving original 4 sts on needle, with RS facing, pick up 3 sts along i-cord. Unwork provisional cast on and slip these 4 sts onto right-hand needle, twisting them around so they appear to be purl sts—*11 sts on needle.* Don't work these last 4 sts. Turn, and work as follows:

Next Row (RS) Knit to last 3 sts; slip 3 pwise wyif.
Next Row (WS) K3; purl to last 3 sts; slip 3 pwise wyif.

Row 1 (RS) K4, ([m1, k1] 4 times), slip 3 pwise wyif—*15 sts on needle.*
Row 2 (WS) K3, ([p1, k1] 4 times), p1; slip 3 pwise wyif.
Row 3 K4, m1, k3, m1, k1, m1, k3, m1, k1, slip 3 pwise wyif—*19 sts on needle.*
Row 4 K3, ([p1, k2] 4 times), p1, slip 3 pwise wyif.
Row 5 K4, m1, k5, m1, k1, m1, k5, m1, k1, slip 3 pwise wyif—*23 sts on needle.*
Row 6 K3, ([p1, k3] 4 times), p1, slip 3 pwise wyif.
Row 7 K4, m1, k7, m1, k1, m1, k7, m1, k1, slip 3 pwise wyif—*27 sts on needle.*
Row 8 K3, ([p1, k4] 4 times), p1, slip 3 pwise wyif.
Row 9 K4, m1, k9, m1, k1, m1, k9, m1, k1, slip 3 pwise wyif—*31 sts on needle.*
Row 10 K3, ([p1, k5] 4 times), p1, slip 3 pwise wyif.

Left Side of Chart A (center sts shown on both pages)

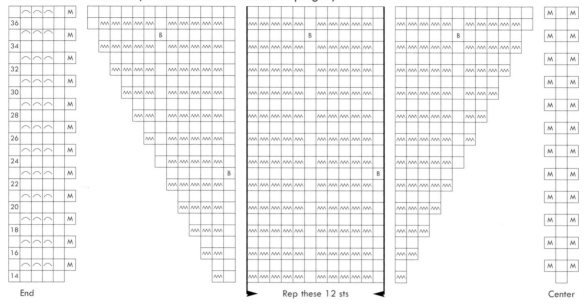

End　　　　　　　　　　Rep these 12 sts　　　　　　　Center

| | knit on RS rows; purl on WS rows. | | slip wyif. | | knit on WS rows. |

Row 11 K4, ([m1, k5, MB, k5, m1, k1] twice), slip 3 pwise wyif—*35 sts on needle.*

Row 12 K3, p2, k5, p1, k5, p3, k5, p1, k5, p2, slip 3 pwise wyif.

Row 13 K4, m1, k13, m1, k1, m1, k13, m1, k1, slip 3 pwise wyif—*39 sts on needle.*

Reading odd-numbered (RS) rows from right to left and even-numbered (WS) rows from left to right, work Rows 14-37 of **Chart A** 5 times, then work Rows 38-85 of **Chart B** once.

I-Cord Cast-Off

Next Row (WS) K3; slip these 3 sts back to left-hand needle; k3; slip these 3 sts back to left hand needle; *K2, ssk; without turning, slide sts to opposite end of needle; bring yarn from behind, tugging gently; rep from * until 3 sts rem; k3. Graft these 3 sts together with i-cord at corner.

FINISHING

Weave in ends. Block gently.

Right Side of Chart A (center sts shown on both pages)

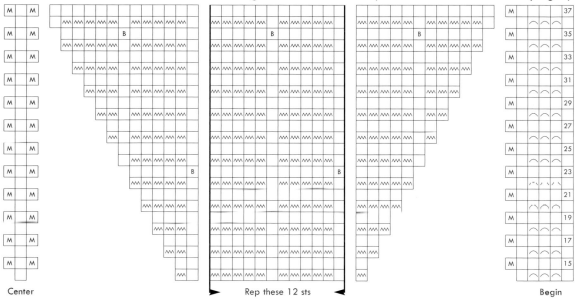

Center   Rep these 12 sts   Begin

B make bobble: k1, yo, k1, yo, k1 in same st; turn; p5; turn; slip 3 sts tog as if to knit; k2tog; pass the 3 slipped sts over the 2 sts knitted tog.

M make one (increase): lift running thread between st just worked and next st; knit into back of this loop.

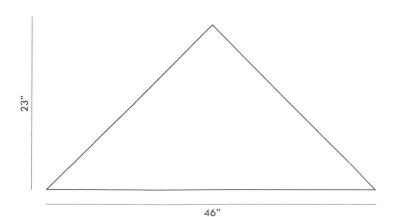

23"

46"

Left Side of Chart B (center sts shown on both pages)

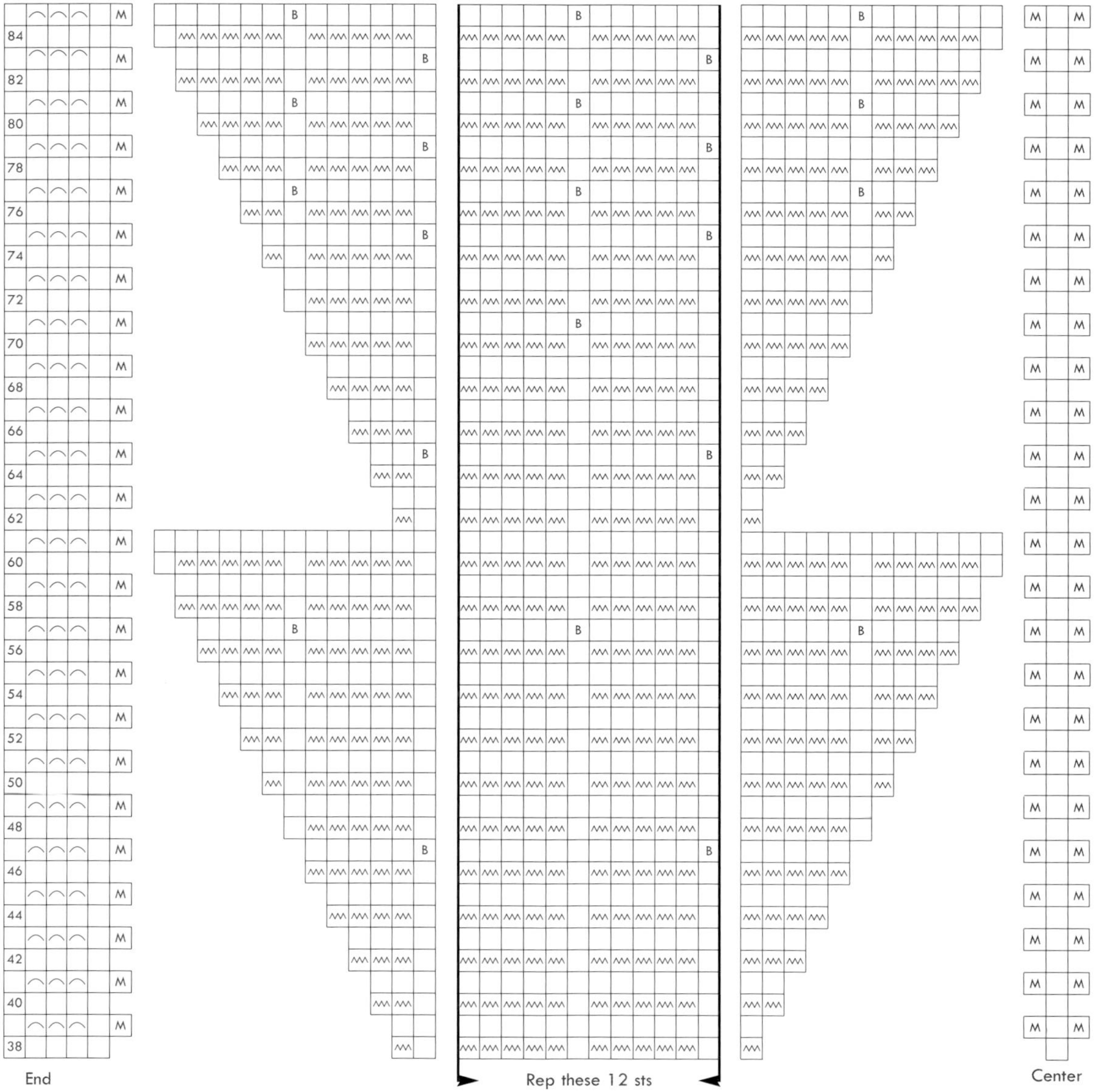

End

Rep these 12 sts

Center

| | knit on RS rows; purl on WS rows. | | slip wyif. | | knit on WS rows. |

Center

Rep these 12 sts

Begin

B — make bobble: k1, yo, k1, yo, k1 in same st; turn; p5; turn; slip 3 sts tog as if to knit; k2tog; pass the 3 slipped sts over the 2 sts knitted tog.

M — make one (increase): lift running thread between st just worked and next st; knit into back of this loop.

Switchback Scarf

bold triangles in lace wool & metal   grace anna farrow

MEASUREMENTS
Width 11½.
Length Approx 115".

YARN
50 grams each of Isager Spinni/Wool 1 in colors #0 (natural white), #2s (lt. natural gray) and #30 (black). 50 grams of Isager Alpaca 1 #16 (chartreuse). 10 grams each of Isager Silk/Stainless Steel in black, brown and gray.

NEEDLES
24" circular US 3 (3.25 mm). One 6" double-pointed US 3. *djust needle size to obtain gauge.*

NOTIONS
6 locking markers or safety pins. 6 long stitch holders or spare yarn.

GAUGE
28 sts = 4".

CONSTRUCTION NOTES
You'll make 6 triangles in the following colorways, then join them together.

SPECIAL TECHNIQUES
I-Cord Bind-Off
K2, slip 1, yo, k1, pass slipped st and yo over, slip sts back to left-hand needle.

Unattached I-Cord
K3, slip sts back to left-hand needle.

3-Needle I-Cord Bind-Off
K2, slip 1, yo, k2tog one st from each needle, pass slipped st and yo over, slip sts back to left-hand needle.

Attached I-Cord Edging
*K2, slip 1, yo, pick up 1 st kwise at scarf edge, pass slipped st and yo over st picked up; slide sts to opposite end of needle; rep from *.

COLORWAYS
Colorway for Triangle A (make 2) Color 1, Spinni #0 (white); Color 2, Silk/Stainless Steel in gray; and color Color 3, Spinni #30 (black). Contrast Color, Alpaca 1 #16 (chartreuse).
Colorway for Triangle B (make 2) Color 1: Spinni #30 (black); Color 2, Silk/Stainless Steel in brown; and Color 3, Spinni #2s (lt. natural gray). Contrast Color, Alpaca 1 #16 (chartreuse).
Colorway for Triangle C (make 2) Color 1, Spinni #2s (lt. natural gray); Color 2, Silk/Stainless Steel in black; and Color 3, Spinni #0 (white). Contrast Color, Alpaca 1 #16 (chartreuse).

MAKE TRIANGLES
Work the following 7 steps for each of the 6 triangles.

1 With Color 1, work the 6 rows of **SET UP**.
2 Continuing with Color 1, work **PATTERN** until there are 23 sts on needle, ending after working a WS row.
3 With Contrast Color, work the 2 rows of **RIDGE PATTERN**.

SWITCHBACK SCARF

4 With Color 2, work **PATTERN** until there are 151 sts on needle, ending after working a WS row.

5 With Contrast Color, work the 2 rows of **RIDGE PATTERN**.

6 With Color 3, work **PATTERN** until there are 215 sts on needle, ending after working a WS row.

7 Place triangle sts onto holder, leaving marker on knitting.

SET UP
With 24" circular US 3, CO 1 st.

Row 1 (RS) K1, p1, k1 into same st—*3 sts on needle*.
Row 2 Purl.
Row 3 ([K1, p1] into first st), m1, k1, m1, ([p1, k1] into last st)—*7 sts on needle*.
Row 4 Purl.
Row 5 K1, m1, k2, m1, k1 (mark this st with locking marker or safety pin), m1, k2, m1, k1—*11 sts on needle*.
Row 6 Purl.

PATTERN
Row 1 (RS) K1, m1, knit to marked st, m1, knit the marked st, m1, knit to last st, m1, k1.
Row 2 Purl.

Rep Rows 1 & 2.

RIDGE PATTERN
Row 1 (RS) K1, m1, knit to marked st, m1, knit the marked st, m1, knit to last st, m1, k1.
Row 2 Knit.

JOIN TRIANGLES
When you've worked all 6 triangles, join them together as follows, moving triangle sts from holders onto needle as needed:

1 With 24" circular US 3 and Contrast Color, CO 3 sts and work **I-Cord Bind-Off** across sts of 1st Triangle A up to, but not including, marked st.

2 Work one row of **Unattached I-Cord**.

3 Work **I-Cord Bind-Off** on marked st of Triangle A.

4 Work one row of **Unattached I-Cord**.

5 Work **3-Needle I-Cord Bind-Off** on rem sts of Triangle A and beginning sts of 1st Triangle B up to, but not including, marked st.

6 Work one row of **Unattached I-Cord**.

7 Work **I-Cord Bind-Off** on marked st of Triangle B.

8 Work one row of **Unattached I-Cord**.

9 Work **3-Needle I-Cord Bind-Off** on rem sts of Triangle B and beginning sts of 1st Triangle C up to, but not including, marked st.

10 Work one row of **Unattached I-Cord**.

11 Work **I-Cord Bind-Off** on marked st of Triangle C.

12 Work one row of **Unattached I-Cord**.

13 Work **3-Needle I-Cord Bind-Off** on rem sts of Triangle C and beginning sts of 2nd Triangle A up to, but not including, marked st.

14 Work one row of **Unattached I-Cord**.

15 Work **I-Cord Bind-Off** on marked st of Triangle A.

16 Work one row of **Unattached I-Cord**.

17 Work **3-Needle I-Cord Bind-Off** on rem sts of Triangle A and beginning sts of 2nd Triangle B up to, but not including, marked st.

18 Work one row of **Unattached I-Cord**.

19 Work **I-Cord Bind-Off** on marked st of Triangle B.

20 Work one row of **Unattached I-Cord**.

21 Work **3-Needle I-Cord Bind-Off** on rem sts of Triangle B and beginning sts of 2nd Triangle C up to, but not including, marked st.

22 Work one row of **Unattached I-Cord**.

23 Work **I-Cord Bind-Off** on marked st of Triangle C.

24 Work one row of **Unattached I-Cord**.

25 Work **I-Cord Bind-Off** on rem sts of Triangle C.

26 BO 3 sts.

FINISH EDGES

With Spinni #0 (white) and 6" double-pointed US 3, CO 3 sts.

1 Beginning at edge where you finished joining the 6 triangles, work **Attached I-Cord Edging** into every row along edge of Triangle C.
2 Change to Spinni #30 (black) and work **Attached I-Cord Edging** into every row along edge of Triangle A.
3 Change to Spinni #2s (lt. natural gray) and work **Attached I-Cord Edging** into every row along edge of Triangle B until you reach the Contrast Color (chartreuse) edge.
4 BO 3 sts.
5 With Spinni #30 (black) and 6" double-pointed US 3, CO 3 sts.

6 Beginning where Contrast Color (chartreuse) edge ends, work **Attached I-Cord Edging** into every row along edge of Triangle A.
7 Change to Spinni #0 (white) and work **Attached I-Cord Edging** into every row along edge of Triangle C.
8 Change to Spinni #2s (lt. natural gray) and work **Attached I-Cord Edging** into every row along edge of Triangle B until you reach the Contrast Color (chartreuse edge).
9 BO 3 sts.

FINISHING

Weave in ends. Block gently.

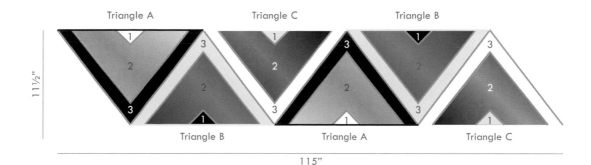

Triangle A   Triangle C   Triangle B

11½"

Triangle B   Triangle A   Triangle C

115"

TUTTO HAND DYES

Ruffled Scarf

ruffled edges for interest on a simple slip stitch　　lis smidt

MEASUREMENTS
6½" wide x 80" long.

YARN
150 grams of Tutto Hand Dyes in Roving Alpaca.

NEEDLES
US 11. *Adjust needle size to obtain gauge.*

GAUGE
17 sts = 4" in pattern.

SCARF
CO 108 sts.

MAKE RUFFLE
Ruffle Row 1 *K2tog; rep from *—*54 sts rem.*
Ruffle Row 2 *K2tog; rep from *—*27 sts rem.*

CONTINUE SCARF
Row 1 *K3, slip 1 pwise wyif; rep from * to last 3 sts; end k3.
Row 2 K1; *slip 1 pwise wyif, k3; rep from * to last 2 sts; end slip 1 pwise wyif, k1.

Rep these 2 rows until scarf measures approx 77-78" and there are approx 10 yards of yarn left over.

MAKE RUFFLE
Ruffle Row 1 Knit into front and back of every st—*54 sts on needle.*
Ruffle Row 2 Knit into front and back of every st—*108 sts on needle.*

Bind off loosely.

FINISHING
Weave in ends. Shape ruffles. Block gently.

6½"

80"

Cozy Socks

colorful country style

gregory courtney

MEASUREMENTS

8" circumference, slightly stretched. Fits most adults, unless foot is extremely wide. Instructions are given to adjust top and foot lengths to fit wearer.

YARN

100 grams of Tutto Donegal Sock and 50 grams of Isager Alpaca 1. Shown in Donegal Sock colorway Indian Paintbrush and Alpaca 1 #25 (red).

Hold 1 strand of Donegal Sock and 1 strand of Alpaca 1 together throughout.

NEEDLES

Set of 5 double-pointed US 4 or 5 (3.5 - 3.75 mm). *Adjust needle size to obtain gauge.*

GAUGE

On US 4 in stockinette st: 24 sts = 4".

2 X 4 RIB PATTERN (MULTIPLE OF 6 STS)

Every Rnd *K2, p2, k4, p2, k2; rep from *.

MAIN PATTERN (MULTIPLE OF 6 STS)

RNDS 1-2 *P1, k1, p2, k1, p2, k1, p2, k1, p1; rep from *.

Rnds 3-8 *K2, p2, k4, p2, k2; rep from *.

Rep Rnds 1-8.

SOCK TOP

With 1 strand of Donegal Sock and 1 strand of Alpaca 1 held together throughout, CO 48 sts. Distribute sts over 4 needles (12 sts per needle). Join, place marker for beginning of rnd and work in the rnd as follows:

Work in **2 X 4 Rib Pattern** for 12 rnds.

Work in **Main Pattern** until top measures desired length—for women, generally 6", for men 8".

HEEL FLAP

Place 24 sts on Needle #1, omit Needle #2, and leave 12 sts each on Needles #3 and #4. Continuing on Needle #1 only for Heel Flap, work back and forth as follows:

Row 1 (RS) *Slip 1 pwise, k1; rep from * to end.
Row 2 (WS) Slip 1 pwise, purl rem sts in row.

Rep these 2 rows for 24 rows, ending with RS facing for next row. There will be 12 slip sts along edges of heel.

TURN THE HEEL

Work short rows as follows:

Row 1 (RS) K12 (to center of heel), k4 sts more, ssk; turn.
Row 2 (WS) Slip 1, p8, p2tog; turn.
Row 3 (RS) Slip 1, k8, ssk; turn.
Row 4 (WS) Slip 1, p8, p2tog; turn.
Rep Rows 3 and 4 until 10 sts rem on needle, ending with RS facing for next row.

Next Row (RS) K5 sts (to middle of heel); this is now the beg of the rnd.

FOOT GUSSET

On Needle #1, k5 heel sts, pick up 13 sts along right side of heel (1 st in each of the 12 slip sts along heel edge and 1 to close the gap between heel and sock top); on Needles #2 and #3, work **2 X 4 Rib Pattern** as established; on Needle #4, pick up 13 sts along left side of heel (1 st in each of the 12 slip sts along heel edge and 1 to close the gap between heel and sock top); work rem 5 heel sts (there are now 18 sts on Needle #1, 12 sts on Needle #2, 12 sts on Needle #3, and 18 sts on Needle #4).

SHAPE THE FOOT GUSSET

Rnd 1 On Needle #1, knit to last 3 sts, k2tog, k1; on Needles #2 and #3, work in **2 X 4 Rib Pattern** as established; on Needle #4, k1, ssk, knit to end.
Rnd 2 On Needle #1, knit all sts; on Needles #2 and #3, work in **2 X 4 Rib Pattern** as established; on Needle #4, knit all sts.

Rep these 2 rnds until there are 12 sts on Needles #1 and #4.

FOOT

On Needles #1 and #4, knit all sts; on Needles #2 and #3, work in **2 X 4 Rib Pattern** as established until entire foot measures about 2" less than length of wearer's foot.

SHAPE THE TOE

Rnd 1 On Needle #1, knit to last 3 sts, k2tog, k1; on Needle #2, k1, ssk, knit to end; on Needle #3, knit to last 3 sts; k2tog, k1; on Needle #4, k1, ssk, knit to end.
Rnd 2 Knit.

Rep these 2 rnds until 28 sts rem.

FINISH THE TOE

Choice 1 Graft the toe (Kitchener st).
Choice 2 (shown) Rep Rnd 1 of toe shaping until 8 sts rem. With tapestry needle, pull thread through rem 8 sts, push needle through hole to inside of sock, pull hole closed, and weave in ends.

Although TUTTO Donegal Sock yarn is machine washable, Isager Alpaca 1 is not. Hand wash gently and lay flat to dry.

Hand Dyed Scarf

mixed color and texture knit horizontally   beatrice smith

MEASUREMENTS
Width 11".
Length 72".

YARN
Color A 50 grams of Tutto Hand Dyes in Brushed Alpaca. *Fuzzy*
Color B 50 grams of Tutto Hand Dyes in Baby Bouclé. *Bumpy*
Color C 50 grams of Isager Alpaca 2. *Plain purple*

Shown in Colors A & B, Mountain Mahogany and Color C, #22 (fuchsia).

NEEDLES
47" or 60" circular US 5 (3.75 mm). *Adjust needle size to obtain gauge.*

GAUGE
17 sts = 4" on US 5 in "broken" garter st.

NOTE Don't break yarns at ends of rows. When necessary, slide work to opposite end of circular needle so correct yarn is in place for next row. This will create an intended "broken" garter st. Carry unused yarns up sides of work.

SCARF
With 1 strand of Color A and 1 strand of Color C held together, CO 308 sts. Using only 1 strand throughout, work as follows:

Rows 1-2 With Color A, knit.
Row 3 With Color B, knit.
Rows 4-5 With Color A, knit.
Rows 6-7 With Color C, knit.

Rep Row 1-7 until scarf measures approx. 11" from CO edge. With 1 strand of Color A and 1 strand of Color C held together, BO loosely.

FINISHING
Weave in ends. Block gently.

11"

72"

Hand Dyed Top

simple square top in broken garter

lis smidt

MEASUREMENTS
Chest 46".
Length 20".

YARN
Color A 100 grams of Tutto Hand Dyes in Baby Bouclé.
Color B 50 grams of TUTTO Hand Dyes in Brushed Alpaca.

NEEDLES
24" circular US 7 (4.5 mm). Crochet hook for finishing (optional). Two spare US 7 needles for joining shoulders. *Adjust needle size to obtain gauge.*

NOTIONS
Two stitch holders or scrap yarn.

GAUGE
16 sts = 4" on US 7 in "broken" garter st.

NOTE Don't break yarns at ends of rows. When necessary, slide work to opposite end of circular needle so correct yarn is in place for next row. This will create an intended "broken" garter st. Carry unused yarns up sides of work.

BACK
CO 92 sts.

Rows 1-2 With Color B, knit.
Row 3 With Color A, knit.

Rep these 3 rows until piece measures 20" from CO edge.

Next Row K24 and place on holder; BO next 44 sts; k24 and place on holder.

FRONT
Work same as for back.

JOIN SHOULDERS
Move right shoulder sts from holders onto separate US 7 needles. With RS's facing each other and WS's facing you, join shoulders using 3-needle bind-off method.

FINISHING
Sew side seams beg at bottom of vest and working upwards, leaving 10" unsewn for armholes. Work single crochet around neck and armhole openings. If you don't crochet, pick up sts along these edges, then BO or leave the edges unfinished. This is a very casual vest!

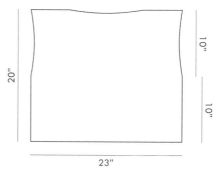

Fitted Raglan Pullover

fitted perfection in luxurious silk/mohair   kristin spurkland

MEASUREMENTS
Chest 32 (36, 40, 44¼)".
Length 22¾ (23, 23½, 24)".
Sleeve 20¼ (20½, 20¾, 20¾)

For best fit, make size that most closely matches or is slightly smaller than your actual chest circumference.

YARN
125 (150, 200, 225) grams of ShibuiKnits Silk Cloud. Garment shown in #40 (cranberry). **Use 1 strand for cast-on, waistband, sleeve cuffs and bind-off. Hold 2 strands together for yoke, body and sleeves.**

NEEDLES
16" and 24" circular US 6 (4 mm) and set of double-pointed US 6. **Optional:** 16" circular US 3 (3.25 mm) or US 4 (3.5 mm) if you choose to cast on using **Double-Needle Cast-On** instructions. *Adjust needle size to obtain guage.*

NOTIONS
Stitch markers. Split-ring markers. Tapestry needle. Stitch holders or waste yarn.

GAUGE
22 sts and 32 rows = 4" in st st on US 6 with 2 strands of yarn held together throughout.

CONSTRUCTION NOTES
Work pullover in the rnd from neck downwards in one piece. After yoke, work front and back together in the rnd, then each sleeve separately in the rnd. The front and back are identical—wear this pullover either way.

DOUBLE-NEEDLE CAST-ON (OPTIONAL)
Measure out a length of yarn as you would for a long-tail cast-on. Hold project needle and smaller needle in right hand between thumb and middle finger, with smaller needle underneath larger needle.

Lay yarn over the two needles, with tail end looped around left thumb from outside of thumb to inside of thumb (holding end down with rem 3 fingers of left hand) and ball end over right index finger.

1 Insert both needles through loop on left thumb going from base of thumb towards tip of thumb.
2 Bring yarn from right hand between the 2 needles from right to left.
3 Push top needle only through loop from right to left and pull taut. Loop yarn over thumb as before.

Rep Steps 1-3 until you've cast on the required number of sts. Pull smaller needle out and work pattern with larger needle only

Double Running Thread Increase (dblinc)
1 Insert left-hand needle tip from front to back under strand that runs between last st on right-hand needle and first st on left-hand needle. Knit into back of this strand.
2 Slip next st pwise.
3 Insert left-hand needle tip from front to back under strand that runs between last st on right-hand needle

and first st on left-hand needle. Knit into back of this strand.

PULLOVER

With 16" circular US 6 and 1 strand of yarn, CO 106 (114, 114, 114) sts loosely using **Double-Needle Cast-On** or the cast-on method of your choice. Place marker for beg of rnd and work in the rnd as follows:

Rnds 1-5 Knit.

From here on, work with 2 strands held together throughout.

Next Rnd (begins in middle of back) K19 (22, 22, 22), knit next st and place a split ring marker in it (**half of back**); k13 (11, 11, 11) (**left sleeve**); knit next st and place a split-ring marker in it, k38 (44, 44, 44), knit next st and place a split ring marker in it (**front**); k13 (11, 11, 11) (**right sleeve**); knit next st and place a split ring marker in it, k19 (22, 22, 22) (**other half of back**).

BEGIN RAGLAN INCREASES

Read this section carefully before beginning. There are exceptions for sizes 40 and 44¼. Be sure to change to 24" circular when sts become too crowded.

All Sizes

Inc Rnd *Knit to marked st, work **dblinc** at marked st; rep from* 3 more times; knit to end of rnd.
Next Rnd Knit.

Rep above 2 rnds 12 (17, 25, 35) more times.

AT SAME TIME—Exception for Size 44¼ Only

Omit sleeve section incs on last 2 of the above inc rnds. Go to **DIVIDE FOR BODY & SLEEVES** after completing all the inc rnds.

Sizes 32, 36 & 40 Continue as Follows

Next Rnd *Knit to marked st, work **dblinc** at marked st; rep from * 3 more times; knit to end of rnd.
Next 3 Rnds Knit.

Rep the above 4 rnds 8 (6, 3) more times. Go to **DIVIDE FOR BODY & SLEEVES**.

AT SAME TIME—Exception for Size 40 Only

Omit sleeve section inc on the next to last of the above inc rnds.

DIVIDE FOR BODY & SLEEVES

All Sizes ([Knit to next marker, knit marked st and remove marker, place next 59 (61, 69, 79) sts on waste yarn; CO 4 sts onto tip of right-hand needle, knit marked st and remove marker] twice); knit to end of rnd—176 (200, 220, 244) body stitches. Do not remove marker at beg of rnd.

Knit until body measures 3" from underarm cast-on.

SHAPE BODY

Dec Set-up Rnd K19 (22, 24, 26); place marker; ssk, k46 (52 58, 66); place marker; k2tog, k38 (44, 48, 52); place marker; ssk, k46 (52, 58, 66); place marker; k2tog, knit to end of rnd.
Next 4 Rnds Knit.
***Next Rnd**: Knit to first marker, ssk, knit to next marker, k2tog, knit to next marker, ssk, knit to next marker, k2tog, knit to end of round.
Next 4 Rnds Knit.

Rep from * 5 more times—*148 (172, 192, 216) sts.* Work without further shaping until body measures 9 (9, 9, 9)" from underarm.

Inc Rnd ([Knit to 1 st past next marker, m1, knit to 1 st before next marker, m1, k1, slip marker] twice); knit to end of rnd.

Next 3 Rnds Knit.

Rep these 4 rnds 9 more times—188 (212, 232, 256) sts. Body measures approx 14 (14, 14, 14)" from underarm after completing body shaping.

WAISTBAND
Break one strand of yarn and work waistband with only 1 strand.

Next 7 Rnds Knit.
Next 2 Rnds *K1, p1; rep from *.
Next Rnd BO in k1, p1 rib, carefully maintaining a flexible, even tension.

SLEEVES
Move sleeve sts from holder or waste yarn onto 16" circular US 6. Holding 2 strands of yarn throughout, pick up 6 sts at underarm, placing a marker between the 3rd and 4th picked-up sts—65 (67, 75, 85) sts. Knit until sleeve measures 1 (1, 2, 2)" from underarm.

SHAPE SLEEVES
***Next 12 (11, 8, 6) Rnds** Knit.
Next Rnd K1, k2tog, knit to last 3 sts, ssk, knit last st.

Rep from * 9 (10, 13, 17) more times, switching to double-pointed needles when sts become too stretched—45 (45, 47, 49) sts.

Work without further shaping until sleeve measures 17½ (17½, 17½, 17½)" from underarm.

From here on, work with only 1 strand throughout.

Next 23 Rnds Knit.
Next Rnd K2tog; knit remaining sts—44 (44, 46, 48) sts.
Next Rnd *K1, p1; rep from *.

BO in k1, p1, maintaining a flexible, even tension.

FINISHING
Weave in ends. Block gently.

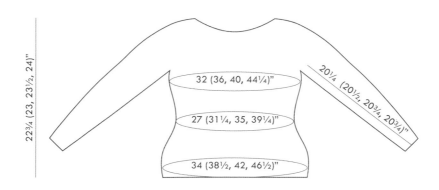

Neck Warmer

a stylish scarf alternative   pamela grossman

MEASUREMENTS
Length 13", not including ribbed ties.
Width 3".
Ribbed Ties Each 14" long.

YARN
100 grams of ShibuiKnits Baby Alpaca DK. Shown in #430 (cranberry).

NEEDLES
US 4 (3.5 mm). *Adjust needle size to obtain gauge.*

GAUGE
40 sts = 4" on US 4 in k1, p1 rib.

SPECIAL ABBREVIATIONS
s2kp Slip next 2 sts together kwise (do this as though you were about to knit 2 sts together, but don't work them; just slip them from the left-hand to right-hand needle, together); knit the next st; pass the 2 slipped sts over the knit st.
p5tog Purl 5 sts together. If you find this to be difficult, try slipping the first 3 sts to the left-hand needle, purl the rem 2 sts together and then pass the 3 slipped sts over the 2 sts purled together.

NECK WARMER
Ribbed Tie
CO 5 sts.

Row 1 (RS) ([P1, k1] twice), p1.
Row 2 (WS) ([K1, p1] twice), k1.

Rep Rows 1-2 until ribbed ties measure 14" from CO edge, ending after working Row 2, then work inc rows as follows:

Row 1 (RS) ([P1, yo] twice), k1, ([yo, p1] twice)—*9 sts on needle.*

NECK WARMER

Row 2 (WS) K3, p3, k3.
Row 3 P2, yo, p1, ([k1, yo] twice), k1, p1, yo, p2—*13 sts on needle.*
Row 4 K4, p5, k4.
Row 5 P2, yo, p2, k2, ([yo, k1] twice), k1, p2, yo, p2—*17 sts on needle.*
Row 6 K5, p7, k5.
Row 7 P2, yo, p1, k1, p1, k7, p1, k1, p1, yo, p2—*19 sts on needle.*
Row 8 (begin bobble) K4, p1, k1, p3, ([k1, yo, k1, yo, k1] in next st), p3, k1, p1, k4—*23 sts on needle.*
Row 9 P2, yo, p2, k1, p1, k3, p5, k3, p1, k1, p2, yo, p2—*25 sts on needle.*

Main Section
Row 10 (end bobble) K5, p1, k1, p3, p5tog, p3, k1, p1, k5—*21 sts on needle.*
Row 11 P2, yo, p2tog, p1, yo, k1, yo, p1, k7, p1, yo, k1, yo, p1, p2tog, yo, p2—*25 sts on needle.*
Row 12 K5, p3, k1 p7, k1, p3, k5.
Row 13 P2, yo, p2tog, p1, ([k1, yo] twice), k1, p1, k2 s2kp, k2, p1, ([k1, yo] twice), k1, p1, p2tog, yo, p2—*27 sts on needle.*
Row 14 K5, ([p5, k1] twice), p5, k5.
Row 15 P2, yo, p2tog, p1, k2, yo, k1, yo, k2, p1, k1 s2kp, k1, p1, k2, yo, k1, yo, k2, p1, p2tog, yo, p2—*29 sts on needle.*
Row 16 K5, p7, k1, p3, k1, p7, k5.
Row 17 P2, yo, p2tog, p1, k7, p1, s2kp, p1, k7, p1, p2tog, yo, p2—*27 sts on needle.*
Row 18 (begin bobble) K5, p3, ([k1, yo, k1, yo, k1] in next st), p3, k1, p1, k1, p3, ([k1, yo, k1, yo, k1] in next st), p3, k5—*35 sts on needle.*
Row 19 P2, yo, p2tog, p1, k3, p5, k3, p1, k1, p1, k3, p5, k3, p1, p2tog, yo, p2.
Row 20 (end bobble) K5, p3, k5tog, p3, k1, p1, k1, p3, p5tog, p3, k5—*27 sts on needle.*
Row 21 P2, yo, p2tog, p1, k7, p1, yo, k1, yo, p1, k7, p1, p2tog, yo, p2—*29 sts on needle.*
Row 22 K5, p7, k1, p3, k1, p7, k5.

Row 23 P2, yo, p2tog, p1, k2, s2kp, k2, p1, ([k1, yo] twice), k1, p1, k2, s2kp, k2, p1, p2tog, yo, p2—*27 sts on needle.*
Row 24 K5, ([p5, k1] twice), p5, k5.
Row 25 P2, yo, p2tog, p1, k1, s2kp, k1, p1, k2, yo, k1, yo, k2, p1, k1, s2kp, k1, p1, p2tog, yo, p2—*25 sts on needle.*
Row 26 K5, p3, k1, p7, k1, p3, k5.
Row 27 P2, yo, p2tog, p1, s2kp p1, k7, p1, s2kp, p1, p2tog, yo, p2—*21 sts on needle.*
Row 28 (begin bobble) K5, p1, k1, p3, ([k1, yo, k1, yo, k1] in next st), p3, k1, p1, k5—*25 sts on needle.*
Row 29 P2, yo, p2tog, p1, k1, p1, k3, p5, k3, p1, k1, p1, p2tog, yo, p2—*25 sts on needle.*

Rep Rows 10–29 four more times, then work dec rows as follows:

Row 1 (end bobble) (WS) K4, s2kp, p3, p5tog, p3, s2kp, k4—*17 sts rem.*
Row 2 (RS) P2, yo, p2tog, p1, k7, p1, p2tog, yo, p2.
Row 3 K5, p7, k5.
Row 4 P2, yo, p2tog, p1, k2, s2kp, k2, p1, p2tog, yo, p2—*15 sts rem.*
Row 5 K5, p5, k5.
Row 6 P1, p2tog, yo, p2tog, k1, s2kp, k1, p2tog, yo, p2tog, p1—*11 sts rem.*
Row 7 K4, p3, k4.
Row 8 P2tog, p2tog, s2kp, p2tog, p2tog—*5 sts rem.*

Ribbed Tie
Row 1 (WS) ([K1, p1] twice), k1.
Row 2 (RS) ([P1, k1] twice), p1.

Rep Rows 1-2 until tie measures 14". BO.

FINISHING
Weave in ends. Block gently.

Yarns Used

ISAGER *www.knitisager.com*
Alpaca 1 (lace/50 grams/437 yards/100% baby alpaca).
Alpaca 2 (fingering/50 grams/270 yards/50% merino wool, 50% baby alpaca).
Highland (fingering/50 grams/305 yards/100% lambswool).
Silk/Stainless Steel (lace/10 grams/220 yards/69% silk, 31% stainless steel).
Spinni/Wool 1 (lace/50 grams/330 yards/100% wool).
Tvinni (fingering/50 grams/280 yards/100% merino lambswool).

MARION FOALE *www.rynyarn.com*
3-Ply Wool (fingering/50 grams/238 yards/100% superwash wool).

SHIBUIKNITS *www.shibuiknits.com*
Baby Alpaca DK (double knitting/100 grams/255 yards/100% baby alpaca).
Silk Cloud (fingering/25 grams/330 yards/60% kid mohair, 40% silk).

TUTTO HAND DYES *www.tuttosantafe.com*
Donegal Sock (fingering/100 grams/463 yards/65% superwash merino wool, 25% nylon, 10% donegal).
Baby Bouclé (double knitting/50 grams/100 yards/35% alpaca, 30% merino wool, 30% bamboo, 5% nylon).
Brushed Alpaca (fingering/50 grams/425 yards/70% baby alpaca, 12% merino wool, 18% nylon).
Roving Alpaca (double knitting/50 grams/120 yards/68% baby alpaca, 10% merino wool, 22% nylon).

Abbreviations

alt = alternate

beg = beginning
BO = bind off

CC = contrast color
cn = cable needle
CO = cast on

dec = decrease(ing)(s)

foll = follow(ing)(s)

inc = increase(ing)(s)

k = knit
kfb = knit into front and back of st (inc)
k1b = knit through back loop
k2tog = knit 2 sts together
kwise = knitwise (as if to knit)

m1 = make 1 st (inc) - lift running thread between st just worked and next st; knit into back of this loop
MC = main color

p = purl
p2tog = purl 2 sts together
patt = pattern
pm = place marker
psso = pass slipped st over st just knitted
pwise = purlwise (as if to purl)

rem = remaining
rep = repeat(ing)(s)
rnd = round(s)
RS = right side

ss(s)k = slip 2 (3) sts (one at a time) kwise; with left-hand needle, knit these 2 (3) sts tog through front of sts
st(s) = stitch(es)
st st = stockinette stitch

tbl = through back loop
tog = together

wyib = with yarn in back
wyif = with yarn in front
WS = wrong side

yo = (inc) yarn over needle (makes a hole or eyelet)

Published & Distributed By TUTTO Santa Fe

Printed in China

ISBN 0-9752931-3-3